The House of Blue Leaves
Bosoms and Neglect

'In Guare's *The House of Blue Leaves*, Artie is a failure, his wife may be schizophrenic, his son wants to kill the Pope, his best friend steals his mistress, and four characters die, one of them murdered before our eyes. Naturally this is comedy, since Guare knows that nothing is funnier than the clash between American dreams and the American way of death . . . a play in touch with darkest intelligence, unsparing in its fundamental concern with public lunacy . . . cold-bloodedly accurate.' *The Village Voice*

'Moving, irreverent farce . . . boldly tragicomic.' *Time*

'John Guare's wild, funny and touching American comedy of the Sixties . . . A witchy brew of distress and absurdity.' *Observer*

Bosoms and Neglect: 'Both shocking and hilarious . . . quite a revelation. Guare presents illness and neurosis in a starkly humorous way that would make Woody Allen blanch. Uncompromising, wicked wit.' *Time Out*

'A vision of insane optimism and everyday insanity.' *Punch*

John Guare lives in New York. His plays include the winner of the 1992 Olivier Best Play Award *Six Degrees of Separation* (Mitzi E Newhouse Theater, Lincoln Center, New York, 1990, Royal Court Theatre, London 1992, transferred to the Comedy Theatre, London, 1992) and *Landscape of the Body* (New York Shakespeare Festival, 1977). His screenplay for Louis Malle's *Atlantic City* won the New York, Los Angeles and National Film Critics Circle awards, as well as an Oscar nomination. A council member of the Dramatists Guild, he was elected in 1989 to the American Academy of Arts and Letters.

John Guare

The House of Blue Leaves
Bosoms and Neglect

Methuen Drama

METHUEN MODERN PLAY

First published in Great Britain 1993
by Methuen Drama
an imprint of Reed Consumer Books Ltd
Michelin House, 81 Fulham Road, London SW3 6RB
and Auckland, Melbourne, Singapore and Toronto

This edition is taken from that published by
Penguin Books USA Inc. 1987 in the Plume edition

ISBN 0–413–67550–5

A CIP catalogue record for this book
is available from the British Library

The front cover image is taken from the poster designed by Chase
Creative Consultants Ltd for the Theatro Technis, London production
of *Bosoms and Neglect* in February 1992.

Printed and bound in Great Britain by
Cox & Wyman Ltd, Cardiff Road, Reading, Berkshire

Contents

THE
HOUSE OF
BLUE
LEAVES

———————

INTRODUCTION

———

The House of Blue Leaves takes place in Sunnyside, Queens, one of the five boroughs of New York City. You have to understand Queens. It was never a borough with its own identity like Brooklyn that people clapped for on quiz shows if you said you came from there. Brooklyn had been a city before it became part of New York, so it always had its own identity. And the Bronx originally had been Jacob Bronck's farm, which at least gives it something personal, and Staten Island is out there on the way to the sea, and, of course, Manhattan is what people mean when they say New York.

Queens was built in the twenties in that flush of optimism as a bedroom community for people on their way up who worked in Manhattan but wanted to pretend they had the better things in life until the inevitable break came and they could make the official move to the Scarsdales and the Ryes and the Greenwiches of their dreams, the pay-off that was the birthright of every American. Queens named its communities Forest Hills, Kew Gardens, Elmhurst, Woodside, Sunnyside, Jackson Heights, Corona, Astoria (after the Astors, of all people). The builders built the apartment houses in mock Tudor or Gothic or Colonial and then named them The Chateau, The El Dorado, Linsley Hall, the Alhambra. We lived first in The East Gate, then moved to The West Gate, then to Hampton Court. And the lobbies had Chippendale furniture and Aztec fireplaces, and the elevators had roman numerals on the buttons.

And in the twenties and thirties and forties you'd move there and move out as soon as you could. Your young married days were over, the promotions came. The ads in the magazines were right. Hallelujah. Queens: a comfortable rest stop, a pleasant rung on the ladder of success, a promise we were promised in some secret dream. (The first paid commercial on American radio was Queensboro Management advertising apartments in Jackson Heights in 1922 on WEAF.) And isn't Manhattan, each day the skyline growing denser and more crenelated, always looming up there in the distance? The elevated subway, the Flushing line, zooms to it, only fourteen minutes from Grand Central Station. Everything you could want you'd find right there in Queens. But the young marrieds become old marrieds, and the children come, but the promotions, the breaks, don't, and you're still there in your bedroom community, your life over the bridge in Manhattan, and the fourteen-minute ride becomes longer every day. Why didn't I get the breaks? I'm right here in the heart of the action, in the bedroom community of the heart of the action, and I live in the El Dorado Apartments and the main street of Jackson Heights has Tudor-topped buildings with pizza slices for sale beneath them and discount radios and discount drugs and discount records and the Chippendale-paneled elevator in my apartment is all carved up with Love To Fuck that no amount of polishing can ever erase. And why do my dreams, which should be the best part of me, why do my dreams, my wants, constantly humiliate me? Why don't I get the breaks? What happened? I'm hip. I'm hep. I'm a New Yorker. The heart of the action. Just a subway ride to the heart of the action. I want to be part of that skyline. I want to blend into those lights. Hey, dreams, I dreamed you. I'm not something you curb a dog for. New York is where it all is. So why aren't I here?

When I was a kid, I wanted to come from Iowa, from New Mexico, to make the final break and leave, say, the flatness of Nebraska and get on that Greyhound and get off that Greyhound at Port Authority and you wave your cardboard suitcase at the sky: I'll Lick You Yet. How do you run away to your dreams when you're already there? I never wanted to be any place in my life but New York. How do you get there when you're there? Fourteen minutes on the Flushing line is a very long distance. And I guess that's what this play is about more than anything else: humiliation. Everyone in the play is constantly being humiliated by their dreams, their loves, their wants, their best parts. People have criticized the play for being cruel or unfeeling. I don't think any play from the Oresteia on down has ever reached the cruelty of the smallest moments in our lives, what we have done to others, what others have done to us. I'm not interested so much in how people survive as in how they avoid humiliation. Chekhov says we must never humiliate one another, and I think avoiding humiliation is the core of tragedy and comedy and probably of our lives.

This is how the play got written: I went to Saint Joan of Arc Grammar School in Jackson Heights, Queens, from 1944 to 1952 (wildly pre-Berrigan years). The nuns would say, If only we could get to Rome, to have His Holiness touch us, just to see Him, capital H, the Vicar of Christ on Earth— Vicar, v.i.c.a.r., Vicar, in true spelling-bee style. Oh, dear God, help me get to Rome, the capital of Italy, and go to that

special little country in the heart of the capital—v.a.t.i.c.a.n.
c.i.t.y.—and touch the Pope. No sisters ever yearned for
Moscow the way those sisters and their pupils yearned for
Rome. And in 1965 I finally got to Rome. Sister Carmela!
Do you hear me? I got here! It's a new Pope, but they're all
the same. Sister Benedict! I'm here! And I looked at the
Rome papers, and there on the front page was a picture of
the Pope. On Queens Boulevard. I got to Rome on the day a
Pope left the Vatican to come to New York for the first
time to plead to the United Nations for peace in the world on
October 4, 1965. He passed through Queens, because you
have to on the way from Kennedy Airport to Manhattan.
Like the Borough of Queens itself, that's how much effect the
Pope's pleas for peace had. The Pope's no loser. Neither is
Artie Shaughnessy, whom *The House of Blue Leaves* is
about. They both have big dreams. Lots of possibilities. The
Pope's just into more real estate.

My parents wrote me about that day that the Pope came
to New York and how thrilled they were, and the letter
caught up with me in Cairo because I was hitching from
Paris to the Sudan. And I started thinking about my parents
and me and why was I in Egypt and what was I doing with
my life and what were they doing with theirs, and that's how
plays get started. The play is autobiographical in the sense
that everything in the play happened in one way or another
over a period of years, and some of it happened in dreams
and some of it could have happened and some of it, luckily,
never happened. But it's autobiographical all the same. My
father worked for the New York Stock Exchange, but he
called it a zoo and Artie in the play is a zoo-keeper. The Billy
in the play is my mother's brother, Billy, a monstrous man
who was head of casting at MGM from the thirties through

the fifties. The Huckleberry Finn episode that begins Act Two is an exact word-for-word reportage of what happened between Billy and me at our first meeting. The play is a blur of many years that pulled together under the umbrella of the Pope's visit.

In 1966 I wrote the first act of the play, and, like some bizarre revenge or disapproval, on the day I finished it my father died. The first act was performed at the O'Neill Theatre Center in Waterford, Connecticut, and I played Artie. The second act came in a rush after that and all the events in that first draft are the same as you'll find in this version. But in 1966 the steam, the impetus for the play, had gone. I wrote another draft of the second act. Another. A fourth. A fifth. A sixth. A director I had been working with was leading the play into abysmal naturalistic areas with all the traps that a set with a kitchen sink in it can have. I was lost on the play until 1969 in London, when one night at the National Theatre I saw Laurence Olivier do *Dance of Death* and the next night, still reeling from it, saw him in Charon's production of *A Flea in Her Ear*. The savage intensity of the first blended into the maniacal intensity of the second, and somewhere in my head *Dance of Death* became the same play as *A Flea in Her Ear*. Why shouldn't Strindberg and Feydeau get married, at least live together, and *The House of Blue Leaves* be their child? For years my two favorite shows had been *Gypsy* and *The Homecoming*. I think the only playwrighting rule is that you have to learn your craft so that you can put on stage plays you would like to see. So I threw away all the second acts of the play, started in again, and, for the first time, understood what I wanted.

Before I was born, just before, my father wrote a song for my mother:

A stranger's coming to our house.
I hope he likes us.
I hope he stays.
I hope he doesn't go away.

I liked them, loved them, stayed too long, and didn't go away. This play is for them.

— JOHN GUARE

1971

CHARACTERS

Artie Shaughnessy
Ronnie Shaughnessy
Bunny Flingus
Bananas Shaughnessy
Corrinna Stroller
Billy Einhorn
Three nuns
A military policeman
The white man

*A cold apartment in Sunnyside, Queens,
New York City.*

October 4, 1965.

MUSIC AND LYRICS BY JOHN GUARE

Warren Lyons and Betty Ann Besch first presented *The House of Blue Leaves* in New York City on February 10, 1971, at the Truck and Warehouse Theatre. The production was directed by Mel Shapiro.

In 1986, a revival of the play was presented at the Lincoln Center Theater by Gregory Mosher, Director, and Bernard Gersten, Executive Producer. The production opened March 19 at the Mitzi Newhouse Theater. It was directed by Jerry Zaks.

CAST

ARTIE SHAUGHNESSY	*John Mahoney*
RONNIE SHAUGHNESSY	*Ben Stiller*
BUNNY FLINGUS	*Stockard Channing*
BANANAS SHAUGHNESSY	*Swoosie Kurtz*
CORRINNA STROLLER	*Julie Hagerty*
THE HEAD NUN	*Patricia Falkenhain*
THE SECOND NUN	*Jane Cecil*
THE LITTLE NUN	*Ann Talman*
THE MILITARY POLICEMAN	*Ian Blackman*
THE WHITE MAN	*Peter J. Downing*
BILLY EINHORN	*Christopher Walken*

On April 29, 1986, the play transferred to the Vivian Beaumont Theater, and on October 14, 1986 to the Plymouth Theater on 45th Street. Christine Baranski took over the role of Bunny. Jack Wallace played Artie. Patricia Clarkson and Faye Grant played Corrinna. Jack Gwaltney assumed the role of Ronnie. Debra Cole played the Little Nun. The understudies were Brian Evers, Kathleen McKiernan, and Melody Somers. The playwright extends a special salute to Danny Aiello, who became Billy Einhorn.

The House of Blue Leaves, directed by Nick Hamm, with Dennis Quilley as Artie Shaughnessy, Nichola McAuliffe as Bananas, Helen Lederer as Bunny, Harry Towb as Billy, Kelly Hunter as Corinna, and John Fitzgerald-Jay as Ronnie, was produced at the Sadler's Wells Theatre, London in October 1988.

PROLOGUE

The stage of the El Dorado Bar & Grill.

While the house lights are still on, and the audience is still being seated, ARTIE SHAUGHNESSY *comes onstage through the curtains, bows, and sits at the upright piano in front of the curtain. He is forty-five years old. He carries sheet music and an opened bottle of beer. He scowls into the wings and then smiles broadly out front.*

ARTIE, *out front, nervous:* My name is Artie Shaughnessy and I'm going to sing you songs I wrote. I wrote all these songs. Words and the music. Could I have some quiet, please? *He sings brightly:*

> Back together again,
> Back together again.
> Since we split up
> The skies we lit up
> Looked all bit up
> Like Fido chewed them,
> But they're back together again.

You can say you knew us when
We were together
Now we're apart,
Thunder and lightning's
Back in my heart,
And that's the weather to be
When you're back together with me.

Into the wings: Could you please turn the lights down?
A spotlight on me? You promised me a spotlight.
Out front: I got a ballad I'm singing and you promised
me a blue spotlight.

The house lights remain on. People are still finding their seats.

ARTIE *plunges on into a ballad sentimentally:*

I'm looking for Something,
I've searched everywhere,
I'm looking for something
And just when I'm there,
Whenever I'm near it
I can see it and hear it,
I'm almost upon it,
Then it's gone.
It seems I'm looking for Something
But what can it be?
I just need a Someone
To hold close to me.
I'll tell you a secret,
Please keep it entre nous,
That Someone
I thought it was you.

Out front: Could you please take your seats and listen? I'm going to sing you a song I wrote at work today and I hope you like it as much as I do. *He plays and sings:*

> Where is the devil in Evelyn?
> What's it doing in Angela's eyes?
> Evelyn is heavenly,
> Angela's in a devil's disguise.
> I know about the sin in Cynthia
> And the hell in Helen of Troy,
> But where is the devil in Evelyn?
> What's it doing in Angela's eyes?
> Oh boy!
> What's it doing in Angela's eyes?

He leaps up from the piano with his sheet music and beer, bows to the audience. Waits for applause. Bows. Waits. Looks. Runs offstage.

The house lights go down.

ACT ONE

─────

The living room of a shabby apartment in Sunnyside, Queens. The room is filled with many lamps and pictures of movie stars and jungle animals.

Upstage center is a bay window, the only window in the room. Across the opening of the bay is a crisscross-barred folding gate of the kind jewelers draw across the front of their stores at night. Outside the window is a fire escape. A small window in the side of the bay is close enough to the gate to be opened or closed by reaching through the bars.

It's late at night and a street lamp beams some light into this dark place through the barred window.

A piano near the window is covered with hundreds of pieces of sheet music and manuscript paper and beer bottles. A jacket, shirt, and pants—the green uniform of a city employee—are draped over the end of the piano nearest the window.

ARTIE *is asleep on the couch, zipped tightly into a sleeping bag, snoring fitfully and mumbling:* Pope Ronnie. Pope Ronnie. Pope Ronald the First. Pope Ronald.

There is a pullman kitchen with its doors open far stage right.

There are three other doors in the room: a front door with many bolts on it, and two doors that lead to bedrooms.

Even though Artie and his family have lived here eighteen years now, there's still an air of transiency to the room as if they had never unpacked from the time they moved in.

Somebody's at the window, climbing down the fire escape. RONNIE, *Artie's eighteen-year-old son, climbs in the window. He gingerly pulls at the folding gate. It's locked. He stands there for a minute, out of breath.*

He's a young eighteen. His hair is cropped close and he wears big glasses. He wears a heavy army overcoat and under that a suit of army fatigue clothes.

He reaches through the bars to his father's trousers, gets the keys out of the pocket, unlocks the lock, comes into the room and relocks the gate behind him, replaces the pants. He tiptoes past his father, who's still snoring and mumbling: Pope Ronnie. Pope Ronnie. Pope Ronnie.

RONNIE *opens the icebox door, careful not to let the light spill all over the floor. He takes out milk and bread.*

The doorbell buzzes.

ARTIE *groans.*

RONNIE *runs into his bedroom.*

Somebody is knocking on the front door and buzzing quickly, quickly like little mosquito jabs.

ARTIE *stirs. He unzips himself from his sleeping bag, runs to the door. He wears ski pajamas. A key fits into the front door. The door shakes.* ARTIE *undoes the six bolts that hold the door locked. He opens the door, dashes back to his bag, and zips himself in.*

BUNNY FLINGUS *throws open the door. The hall behind her*

is brilliantly lit. She is a pretty, pink, slightly plump, electric woman in her late thirties. She wears a fur-collared coat and plastic booties, and two Brownie cameras on cords clunking against a pair of binoculars.

At the moment she is freezing, uncomfortable, and furious.

She storms to the foot of the couch.

BUNNY: You know what your trouble is? You got no sense of history. You know that? Are you aware of that? Lock yourself up against history, get drowned by the whole tide of human events. Sleep it away in your bed. Your bag. Zip yourself in, Artie. The greatest tide in the history of the world is coming in today, so don't get your feet wet.

ARTIE, *picking up his glow-in-the-dark alarm:* It's quarter-to-five in the morning, Bunny—

BUNNY: Lucky for you I got a sense of history. *She sits on the edge of the couch, picks up the newspaper on the floor.* You finished last night's? Oooo, it's freezing out there. Breath's coming out of everybody's mouth like a balloon in a cartoon. *She rips the paper into long shreds and stuffs it down into the plastic booties she wears.*

People have been up for hours. Queens Boulevard—lined for blocks already! Steam coming out of everybody's mouth! Cripples laid out in the streets in stretchers with ear muffs on over their bandages. Nuns—you never seen so many nuns in your life! Ordinary people like you and me in from New Jersey and Connecticut and there's a lady even drove in from Ohio—Ohio!—just for today! She drove four of the most crippled people in Toledo. They're stretched out in the gutter waiting for the sun to come out so they can start snapping pictures. I haven't seen so many people, Artie, so excited since the premiere of *Cleopatra*. It's that big. Breathe! There's miracles in the air!

ARTIE: It's soot, Bunny. Polluted air.

BUNNY: All these out-of-staters driving in with cameras and thermos bottles and you live right here and you're all zipped in like a turtle. Miss Henshaw, the old lady who's the check-out girl at the A & P who gyps everybody—her nephew is a cop and she's saving us two divine places right by the curb. You're not the only one with connections. But she can't save them forever. Oh God, Artie, what a morning! You should see the stars!!! I know all the stars from the time I worked for that astronomer and you should see Orion—O'Ryan: the Irish constellation—I haven't looked up and seen stars in years! I held my autograph book up and let Jupiter shine on it. Jupiter and Venus and Mars. They're all out! You got to come see Orion. He's the hunter and he's pulling his arrow back so tight in the sky like a Connect-the-Dots picture made up of all these burning planets. If he ever lets that arrow go, he'll shoot all the other stars out of the sky—what a welcome for the Pope!

And right now, the Pope is flying through that star-filled sky, bumping planets out of the way, and he's asleep dreaming of the mobs waiting for him. When famous people go to sleep at night, it's us they dream of, Artie. The famous ones—they're the real people. We're the creatures of their dreams. You're the dream. I'm the dream. We have to be there for the Pope's dream. Look at the light on the Empire State Building swirling around and around like a burglar's torch looking all through the sky— Everybody's waiting, Artie—everybody!

ARTIE, *angry*: What I want to know is who the hell is paying for this wop's trip over here anyway—

BUNNY, *shocked:* Artie! *She reaches through the bars to close the window.* Ssshhh—they'll hear you—

ARTIE: I don't put my nickels and dimes in Sunday collections to pay for any dago holiday—flying over here with his robes and gee-gaws and bringing his buddies over when I can't even afford a trip to Staten Island—

BUNNY, *puzzled:* What's in Staten Island?

ARTIE: Nothing! But I couldn't even afford a nickel ferry-boat ride. I known you two months and can't even afford a present for you—a ring—

BUNNY: I don't need a ring—

ARTIE: At least a friendship ring— *He reaches in his sleeping bag and gets out a cigarette and matches and an ashtray.*

BUNNY, *rubbing his head:* I'd only lose it—

ARTIE, *pulling away:* And this guy's flying over here—not tourist—oh no—

BUNNY, *suspicious of his bitterness:* Where'd you go last night?

ARTIE, *back into his bag:* You go see the Pope. Tell him hello for me.

BUNNY: You went to that amateur night, didn't you—

ARTIE, *signaling toward the other room:* Shut up—she's inside—

BUNNY: You went to the El Dorado Bar Amateur Night, didn't you. I spent two months building you up to be something and you throw yourself away on that drivel—

ARTIE: They talked all the way through it—

BUNNY: Did you play them "Where's the Devil in Evelyn?"?

ARTIE: They talked and walked around all through it—

BUNNY: I wish I'd been there with you. You know what I would've said to them?

To us: The first time I heard "Mairzy Doats" I realized I am listening to a classic. I picked off "Old Black Magic" and "I Could've Danced All Night" as classics the min-

ute I heard them. *She recites:* "Where is the devil in Evelyn? What's it doing in Angela's eyes?" I didn't work in
Macy's Music Department for nix. I know what I'm talking about.

To Artie: That song is a classic. You've written yourself a
classic.

ARTIE: I even had to pay for my own beers.

BUNNY: Pearls before swine. Chalk it up to experience.

ARTIE: The blackboard's getting kind of filled up. I'm too old
to be a young talent.

BUNNY *opens the window through the bars:* Smell the bread—

ARTIE: Shut the window—it's freezing and you're letting all
the dirt in—

BUNNY: Miss Henshaw's saving us this divine place right by
the cemetery so the Pope will have to slow down—

ARTIE: Nothing worse than cold dirt—

The other bedroom door opens and BANANAS SHAUGHNESSY, *a
sick woman in a nightgown, looks at them. They don't see her.*

BUNNY, *ecstatically:* And when he passes by in his limousine,
I'll call out, "Your Holiness, marry us—the hell with peace
to the world—bring peace to us." And he won't hear me
because bands will be playing and the whole city yelling,
but he'll see me because I been eyed by the best of them,
and he'll nod and I'll grab your hand and say, "Marry us,
Pope," and he'll wave his holy hand and all the emeralds
and rubies on his fingers will send Yes beams. In a way,
today's my wedding day. I should have something white
at my throat! Our whole life is beginning—my life—our
life—and we'll be married and go out to California and
Billy will help you. You'll be out there with the big shots—
out where you belong—not in any amateur nights in bars

on Queens Boulevard. Billy will get your songs in movies. It's not too late to start. With me behind you! Oh, Artie, the El Dorado Bar will stick up a huge neon sign flashing onto Queens Boulevard in a couple of years flashing "Artie Shaughnessy Got Started Here." And nobody'll believe it. Oh, Artie, tables turn.

BANANAS *closes the door.*
ARTIE *gets out of his bag. He sings thoughtfully:*

> Bridges are for burning
> Tables are for turning—

He turns on all the lights. He pulls Bunny by the pudgy arm over to the kitchen.

ARTIE: I'll go see the Pope—
BUNNY, *hugging him:* Oh, I love you!
ARTIE: I'll come if—
BUNNY: You said you'll come. That is tantamount to a promise.
ARTIE: I will if—
BUNNY: Tantamount. Tantamount. You hear that? I didn't work in a law office for nix. I could sue you for breach.
ARTIE, *seductively:* Bunny?
BUNNY, *near tears:* I know what you're going to say—
ARTIE, *opening a ketchup bottle under her nose:* Cook for me?
BUNNY, *in a passionate heat:* I knew it. I knew it.
ARTIE: Just breakfast.
BUNNY: You bend my arm and twist my heart but I got to be strong.
ARTIE: I'm not asking any ten-course dinner.

To get away from his plea, BUNNY *runs over to the piano, where his clothes are draped.*

BUNNY: Just put your clothes on over the ski p.j.'s I bought you. It's thirty-eight degrees and I don't want you getting your pneumonia back—

ARTIE, *holding up two eggs:* Eggs, baby. Eggs right here.

BUNNY, *holding out his jingling trousers:* Rinse your mouth out to freshen up and come on let's go?

ARTIE, *seductively:* You boil the eggs and pour lemon sauce over—

BUNNY, *shaking the trousers at him:* Hollandaise. I know hollandaise. *She plops down with the weight of the temptation, glum.* It's really cold out, so dress warm— Look, I stuffed the *New York Post* in my booties—plastic just ain't as warm as it used to be.

ARTIE: And you pour the hollandaise over the eggs on English muffins—and then you put the grilled ham on top— I'm making a scrapbook of all the foods you tell me you know how to cook and then I go through the magazines and cut out pictures of what it must look like. *He gets the scrapbook.* Look—veal parmagina—eggplant meringue.

BUNNY: I cooked that for me last night. It was so good I almost died.

ARTIE *sings, as Bunny takes the book and looks through it with great despair:*

> If you cooked my words
> Like they was veal
> I'd say I love you
> For every meal.
> Take my words,

> Garlic and oil them,
> Butter and broil them,
> Sauté and boil them—
> Bunny, let me eat you!

He speaks: Cook for me?

BUNNY: Not till after we're married.

ARTIE: You couldn't give me a little sample right now?

BUNNY: I'm not that kind of girl. I'll sleep with you anytime you want. Anywhere. In two months I've known you, did I refuse you once? Not once! You want me to climb in the bag with you now? Unzip it—go on—unzip it— Give your fingers a smack and I'm flat on my back. I'll sew those words into a sampler for you in our new home in California. We'll hang it right by the front door. Because, Artie, I'm a rotten lay and I know it and you know it and everybody knows it—

ARTIE: What do you mean? Everybody knows it—

BUNNY: I'm not good in bed. It's no insult. I took that sex test in the *Reader's Digest* two weeks ago and I scored twelve. Twelve, Artie! I ran out of that dentist office with tears gushing out of my face. But I face up to the truth about myself. So if I cooked for you now and said I won't sleep with you till we're married, you'd look forward to sleeping with me so much that by the time we did get to that motel near Hollywood, I'd be such a disappointment, you'd never forgive me. My cooking is the only thing I got to lure you on with and hold you with. Artie, we got to keep some magic for the honeymoon. It's my first honeymoon and I want it to be so good, I'm aiming for two million calories. I want to cook for you so bad I walk by the A & P, I get all hot jabs of chili powder inside my thighs . . . but I can't till we get those tickets to California safe in my purse, till Billy knows we're coming, till I got that ring right on my cooking finger. . . . Don't tempt me . . . I love you . . .

ARTIE, *beaten:* Two eggs easy over?

BUNNY *shakes her head No:* And I'm sorry last night went sour . . .

ARTIE *sits down, depressed:* They made me buy my own beers . . .

BANANAS, *calling from the bedroom:* Is it light? Is it daytime already?

ARTIE *and* BUNNY *look at each other.*

BUNNY: I'll pour you cornflakes.

ARTIE, *nervous:* You better leave.

BUNNY, *standing her ground:* A nice bowlful?

ARTIE: I don't want her to know yet.

BUNNY: It'll be like a coming attraction.

ARTIE, *pushing her into the kitchen:* You're a tease, Bunny, and that's the worst thing to be. *He puts on his green shirt and pants over his pajamas.*

BANANAS *comes out of the bedroom. She's lived in her night-gown for the last six months. She's in her early forties and has been crying for as long as she's had her nightgown on. She walks uncertainly, as if hidden barriers lay scattered in her path.*

BANANAS: Is it morning?

ARTIE, *not knowing how to cope wth her:* Go back to bed.

BANANAS: You're dressed and it's so dark. Did you get an emergency call? Did the lion have babies yet?

ARTIE, *checking that the gate is locked:* The lioness hasn't

dropped yet. The jaguar and the cheetah both still waiting. The birds still on their eggs.

BANANAS: Are you leaving to get away from me? Tell me?
The truth? You hate me. You hate my looks—my face—
my clothes—you hate me. You wish I was fatter so there'd
be more of me to hate. You hate me. Don't say that! You
love me. I know you love me. You love me. Well, I don't
love you. How does that grab you? *She is shaking vio-
lently.*

ARTIE *takes pills from the piano and holds her, forcing the
pills in her mouth. He's accepted this as one of the natural
facts of his life. There is no violence in the action. Her body
shakes. The spasms stop. She's quiet for a long time. He walks
over to the kitchen.* BUNNY *kisses the palm of his hand.*

BANANAS: For once could you let my emotions come out? If I
laugh, you give me a pill. If I cry, you give me a pill ...
no more pills ... I'm quiet now....

ARTIE *comes out of the kitchen and pours two pills into his
hand. He doesn't like to do this.*

BANANAS *smiles:* No! No more—look at me—I'm a peaceful
forest, but I can feel all the animals have gone back into
hiding and now I'm very quiet. All the wild animals have
gone back into hiding. But once—once let me have an
emotion? Let the animals come out? I don't like being
still, Artie. It makes me afraid ...
    Brightly: How are you this morning? Sleep well?
You were out late last night. I heard you come in and
moved over in the bed. Go back to bed and rest. It's still
early ... come back to bed ...

ARTIE, *finishing dressing:* The Pope is coming today and I'm
  going to see him.

BANANAS: The Pope is coming here?

ARTIE: Yes, he's coming here. We're going to kick off our shoes
  and have a few beers and kick the piano around. *Gently,
  as if to a child:* The Pope is talking to the UN about Vietnam. He's coming over to stop the war so Ronnie won't
  have to go to Vietnam.

BANANAS: Three weeks he's been gone. How can twenty-one
  days be a hundred years?

ARTIE, *to the audience:* This woman doesn't understand. My
  kid is charmed. He gets greetings to go to basic training
  for Vietnam and the Pope does something never done
  before. He flies out of Italy for the first time *ever* to stop
  the war. Ronnie'll be home before you can say Jake Ra-
  binowitz. Ronnie—what a kid—a charmed life . . .

BANANAS: I can't go out of the house . . . my fingernails are all
  different lengths. I couldn't leave the house. . . . Look—I
  cut this one just yesterday and look how long it is
  already . . . but this one . . . I cut it months ago right down
  to the quick and it hasn't moved that much. I don't
  understand that. . . . I couldn't see the Pope. I'd embarrass him. My nails are all different. I can feel them
  growing . . . they're connected to my veins and heart and
  pulling my insides out my fingers. *She is getting hysterical.*

ARTIE *forces pills down her mouth. She's quiet. She smiles at
  him. Artie's exhausted, upset. He paces up and down in front
  of her, loathing her.*

ARTIE: The Pope takes one look at you standing on Queens
  Boulevard, he'll make the biggest U-turn you ever saw

right back to Rome. *Angry:* I dreamed last night Ronnie was the Pope and he came today and all the streets were lined with everybody waiting to meet him—and I felt like Joseph P. Kennedy, only bigger, because the Pope is a bigger draw than any President. And it was raining everywhere but on him and when he saw you and me on Queens Boulevard, he stopped his glass limo and I stepped into the bubble, but you didn't. He wouldn't take you.

BANANAS: He would take me!

ARTIE, *triumphant:* Your own son denied you. Slammed the door in your face and you had open-toe shoes on and the water ran in the heels and out the toes like two Rin Tin Tins taking a leak—and Ronnie and I drove off to the UN and the war in Vietnam stopped and he took me back to Rome and canonized me—made me a Saint of the Church and in charge of writing all the hymns for the Church. A hymn couldn't be played unless it was mine and the whole congregation sang "Where Is the Devil in Evelyn?" but they made it sound like monks singing it— You weren't invited, Bananas. Ronnie loved only me. . . . *He finds himself in front of the kitchen. He smiles at Bunny.* What a dream . . . it's awful to have to wake up. For my dreams, I need a passport and shots. I travel the whole world.

BUNNY, *whispering:* I dreamed once I met Abraham Lincoln.

ARTIE: Did you like him?

BUNNY: He was all right. *She opens a jar of pickles and begins eating them.*

BANANAS *sees Bunny's fur coat by Ronnie's room. She opens the front door and throws the coat into the hall. She closes the door behind her.*

BANANAS: You know what I dream? I dream I'm just waking
   up and I roam around the house all day crying because
   of the way my life turned out. And then I do wake up
   and what do I do? Roam around the house all day crying
   about the way my life turned out.

An idea comes to ARTIE. *He goes to the piano and sings:*

> The day that the Pope came to New York
> The day that the Pope came to New York,
> It really was comical,
> The Pope wore a yarmulke
> The day that the Pope came to New York.

BANANAS: Don't be disrespectful.

She gets up to go to the kitchen. ARTIE *rushes in front of her
and blocks her way.* BUNNY *pushes herself against the icebox
trying to hide; she's eating a bowl of cornflakes.*

ARTIE: Stay out of the kitchen. I'll get your food—
BANANAS: Chop it up in small pieces . . .
BUNNY, *in a loud, fierce whisper:* Miss Henshaw cannot re-
   serve our places indefinitely. Tantamount to theft is holding a place other people could use. Tantamount. Her
   nephew the cop could lock us right up. Make her go back
   to bed.

ARTIE *fixes Bananas's food on a plate.*
BANANAS *sits up on her haunches and puts her hands, palm
downward, under her chin.*

BANANAS: Hello, Artie!

ARTIE: You're going to eat like a human being.

BANANAS: Woof? Woof?

ARTIE: Work all day in a zoo. Come home to a zoo.

He takes a deep breath. He throws her the food. She catches it in her mouth. She rolls on her back.

BANANAS: I like being animals. You know why? I never heard of a famous animal. Oh, a couple of Lassies—an occasional Trigger—but, by and large, animals weren't meant to be famous.

ARTIE *storms into the kitchen.*

BUNNY: What a work of art is a dog. How noble in its thought —how gentle in its dignity—

ARTIE *buries his head against the icebox.*

BANANAS, *smiling out front:* Hello. I haven't had a chance to welcome you. This is my home and I'm your hostess and I should welcome you. I wanted to say Hello and I'm glad you could come. I was very sick a few months ago. I tried to slash my wrists with spoons. But I'm better now and glad to see people. In the house. I couldn't go out. Not yet. Hello. *She walks the length of the stage, smiling at the audience, at us. She has a beautiful smile.*

BUNNY *comes out of the kitchen down to the edge of the stage.*

BUNNY, *to us:* You know what my wish is? The priest told us last Sunday to make a wish when the Pope rides by.

When the Pope rides by, the wish in my heart is gonna
knock the Pope's eye out. It is braided in tall letters, all
my veins and arteries and aortas are braided into the wish
that she dies pretty soon. *She goes back to the kitchen.*

BANANAS, *who has put a red mask on her head:* I had a vision
—a nightmare—I saw you talking to a terrible fat woman
with newspapers for feet—and she was talking about
hunters up in the sky and that she was a dream and you
were a dream ... *She crosses to the kitchen, pulls the mask
down over her eyes, and comes up behind Bunny:* Hah!!!

BUNNY *screams in terror and runs into the living room.*

BUNNY: I am not taking insults from a sick person. A healthy
person can call me anything they want. But insults from
a sickie—a sicksicksickie—I don't like to be degraded. A
sick person has fumes in their head—you release poison
fumes and it makes me sick—dizzy—like riding the back
of a bus. No wonder Negroes are fighting so hard to be
freed, riding in the back of buses all those years. I'm
amazed they even got enough strength to stand up
straight. . . . Where's my coat? Artie, where's my coat?
My binox and my camera? *To Bananas:* What did you
do with my coat, Looney Tunes?

ARTIE *has retrieved the coat from the hallway.*

BUNNY: You soiled my coat! This coat is soiled! Arthur, are
you dressed warm? Are you coming?

ARTIE, *embarrassed:* Bananas, I'd like to present—I'd like you
to meet—this is Bunny Flingus.

BUNNY: You got the ski p.j.'s I bought you on underneath?
You used to go around freezing till I met you. I'll teach

you how to dress warm. I didn't work at ski lodges for
nothing. I worked at Aspen.

BANANAS *thinks it over a moment:* I'm glad you're making
friends, Artie. I'm no good for you.

BUNNY, *taking folders out of her purse, to Bananas:* I might
as well give these to you now. Travel folders to Juarez.
It's a simple procedure—you fly down to Mexico—wet-
back lawyer meets you—sign a paper—jet back to little
old N.Y.

ARTIE: Bunny's more than a friend, Bananas.

BUNNY: Play a little music—"South of the Border"—divorce
Meheeco style!—

ARTIE: Would you get out of here, Bunny. I'll take care of this.

BANANAS *sings hysterically, without words, "South of the
Border."*

BUNNY: I didn't work in a travel agency for nix, Arthur.

ARTIE: Bunny!

BUNNY: I know my way around.

BANANAS *stops singing.*

ARTIE, *taking the folders from Bunny:* She can't even go to
the incinerator alone. You're talking about Mexico—

BUNNY: I know these sick wives. I've seen a dozen like you in
movies. I wasn't an usher for nothing. You live in wheel
chairs just to hold your husband and the minute your
husband's out of the room, you're hopped out of your
wheel chair doing the Charleston and making a general
spectacle of yourself. I see right through you. Tell her,
Artie. Tell her what we're going to do.

ARTIE: We're going to California, Bananas.

BUNNY: Bananas! What a name!

BANANAS: A trip would be nice for you ...

BUNNY: What a banana—

BANANAS: You could see Billy. . . . I couldn't see Billy. . . .
   Almost laughing: I can't see anything ...

ARTIE: Not a trip.

BUNNY: To live. To live forever.

BANANAS: Remember the time we rode up in the elevator with
   Bop Hope? He's such a wonderful man.

ARTIE: I didn't tell you this, Bunny. Last week, I rode out to
   Long Island. *To Bananas, taking her hand:* You need
   help. We—*I* found a nice hosp ... By the sea ... by the
   beautiful sea ... It's an old estate and you can walk from
   the train station and it was raining and the roads aren't
   paved so it's muddy, but by the road where you turn into
   the estate, there was a tree with blue leaves in the rain—
   I walked under it to get out of the rain and also because
   I had never seen a tree with blue leaves and I walked
   under the tree and all the leaves flew away in one big
   round bunch—just lifted up, leaving a bare tree. Whoosh.
   . . . It was birds. Not blue leaves but birds, waiting to go
   to Florida or California ... and all the birds flew to another tree a couple of hundred feet off and that bare tree
   blossomed—snap! like that—with all these blue very
   quiet leaves. . . . You'll like the place, Bananas. I talked
   to the doctor. He had a mustache. You like mustaches.
   And the Blue Cross will handle a lot of it, so we won't
   have to worry about expense. . . . You'll like the place
   . . . a lot of famous people have had crackdowns there,
   so you'll be running in good company.

BANANAS: Shock treatments?

ARTIE: No. No shock treatments.

BANANAS: You swear?

BUNNY: If she needs them, she'll get them.

ARTIE: I'm handling this my way.

BUNNY: I'm sick of you kowtowing to her. Those poison fumes that come out of her head make me dizzy—suffering—look at her—what does she know about suffering...

BANANAS: Did you read in the paper about the bull in Madrid who fought so well they didn't let him die? They healed him, let him rest before they put him back in the ring, again and again and again. I don't like the shock treatments, Artie. At least the concentration camps—I was reading about them, Artie—they put the people in the ovens and never took them out—but the shock treatments —they put you in the oven and then they take you out and then they put you in and then they take you out ...

BUNNY: Did you read *Modern Screen* two months ago? I am usually not a reader of film magazines, but the cover on it reached right up and seduced my eye in the health club. It was a picture like this—*she clutches her head*— and it was called "Sandra Dee's Night of Hell." Did you read that by any happpenstance? Of course you wouldn't read it. You can't see anything. You're ignorant. Not you. Her. The story told of the night before Sandra Dee was to make her first movie and her mother said, "Sandra, do you have everything you need?" And she said— snapped back, real fresh-like—"Leave me alone, Mother. I'm a big girl now and don't need any help from you." So her mother said, "All right, Sandra, but remember I'm always here." Well, her mother closed the door and Sandra could not find her hair curlers anywhere and she was too proud to go to her mom and ask her where they were—

ARTIE: Bunny, I don't understand.

BUNNY: Shut up, I'm not finished yet—and she tore through the house having to look her best for the set tomorrow because it was her first picture and her hair curlers were nowhere! Finally at four in the A.M., her best friend, Annette Funicello, the former Mouseketeer, came over and took the hair curlers out of her very own hair and gave them to Sandra. Thus ended her night of hell, but she had learned a lesson. Suffering—you don't even know the meaning of suffering. You're a nobody and you suffer like a nobody. I'm taking Artie out of this environment and bringing him to California while Billy can still do him some good. Get Artie's songs—his music—into the movies.

ARTIE: I feel I only got about this much life left in me, Bananas. I got to use it. These are my peak years. I got to take this chance. You stay in your room. You're crying. All the time. Ronnie's gone now. This is not a creative atmosphere. . . . Bananas, I'm too old to be a young talent.

BANANAS: I never stopped you all these years . . .

BUNNY: Be proud to admit it, Artie. You were afraid till I came on the scene. Admit it with pride.

ARTIE: I was never afraid. What're you talking about?

BUNNY: No man takes a job feeding animals in the Central Park Zoo unless he's afraid to deal with humans.

ARTIE: I walk right into the cage! What do you mean?

BUNNY: Arthur, I'm trying to talk to your wife. Bananas, I want to be sincere to you and kind.

ARTIE: I'm not afraid of nothing! Put my hand right in the cage—

BUNNY, *sitting down beside Bananas, speaks to her as to a child:* There's a beautiful book of poems by Robert Graves. I never read the book because the title is so beautiful there's no need to read the book: "Man Does.

Woman Is." Look around this apartment. Look at Artie.
Look at him.

ARTIE, *muttering:* I been with panthers.

BUNNY, *with great kindness:* I've never met your son, but—
no insult to you, Artie—but I don't want to. Man does.
What does Artie do? He plays the piano. He creates.
What are you? What is Bananas? Like he said before
when you said you've been having nightmares. Artie said,
"You been looking in the mirror?" Because that's what
you are, Bananas. Look in the mirror.

ARTIE *is playing the piano*—"Where Is the Devil in Evelyn?"

BUNNY: *Man Does. Woman Is.* I didn't work in a lending
library for nothing.

ARTIE: I got panthers licking out of my hands like goddam
pussycats.

BUNNY: Then why don't you ever call Billy?

ARTIE *stops playing:* I got family obligations.

BANANAS, *at the window:* You could take these bars down.
I'm not going to jump.

BUNNY: You're afraid to call Billy and tell him we're coming
out.

BANANAS, *dreamy:* I'd like to jump out right in front of the
Pope's car.

ARTIE: Panthers lay right on their backs and I tickle their arm-
pits. You call me afraid? Hah!

BANANAS: He'd take me in his arms and bless me.

BUNNY: Then call Billy now.

ARTIE: It's the middle of the night!

BUNNY: It's only two in the morning out there now.

ARTIE: Two in the morning is the middle of the night!

BUNNY: In Hollywood! Come off it, he's probably not even in

yet—they're out there frigging and frugging and swing-
ing and eating and dancing. Since Georgina died, he's
probably got a brace of nude starlets splashing in the pool.

ARTIE: I can't call him. He's probably not even in yet—

BUNNY: I don't even think you know him.

ARTIE: Don't know him!

BUNNY: You've been giving me a line—your best friend—big
Hollywood big shot—you don't even know him—

ARTIE: Best friends stay your best friends precisely because you
don't go calling them in the middle of the night.

BUNNY: You been using him—dangling him over my head—
big Hollywood big-shot friend, just to take advantage of
me—just to get in bed with me— Casting couches! I
heard about them—

ARTIE: That's not true!

BUNNY: And you want me to cook for you! I know the score,
baby. I didn't work in a theatrical furniture store for
nothing!

She tries to put her coat on to leave. He pulls it off her.
If you can't call your best friends in the middle of the
night, then who can you call—taking advantage of me in
a steam bath—

BANANAS, *picking up the phone:* You want me to get Billy on
the phone?

ARTIE: You stay out of this!

BANANAS: He was always my much better friend than yours,
Artie.

ARTIE: Your friend! Billy and I only went to kindergarten
together, grammar school together, high school together
till his family moved away—Fate always kept an eye out
to keep us friends. *He sings:*

If you're ever in a jam, here I am.

BANANAS *sings:*

Friendship.

ARTIE *sings:*

If you're ever up a tree, just phone me.

ARTIE *turns to us exuberantly:* He got stationed making training movies and off each reel there's what they call leader
—undeveloped film—and he started snipping that leader
off, so by the time we all got discharged, he had enough
film spliced up to film Twenty Commandments. He
made his movie right here on the streets of New York
and Rossellini was making his movies in Italy, only Billy
was making them here in America and better. He sold
everything he had and he made *Conduct of Life* and it's
still playing in museums. It's at the Museum of Modern
Art next week—and Twentieth Century–Fox signed him
and MGM signed him—they both signed him to full
contracts—the first time anybody ever got signed by two
studios at once. . . . You only knew him about six months'
worth, Bananas, when he was making the picture. And
everybody in that picture became a star and Billy is still
making great pictures.

BUNNY: In his latest one, will you ever forget that moment
when Doris Day comes down that flight of stairs in that
bathrobe and thinks Rock Hudson is the plumber to fix
her bathtub and in reality he's an atomic scientist.

BANANAS: I didn't see that . . .

ARTIE, *mocking:* Bananas doesn't go out of the house . . .

BUNNY, *stars in her eyes:* Call him, Artie.

ARTIE: He gets up early to be on the set. I don't want to wake him up—

BUNNY: Within the next two years, you could be out there in a black tie waiting for the lady—Greer Garson—to open the envelope and say as the world holds its breath—"And the winner of the Oscar for this year's Best Song is—" *She rips a travel folder very slowly.*

ARTIE, *leaning forward:* Who is it? Who won?

BUNNY: And now Miss Mitzi Gaynor and Mr. Franco Corelli of the Metropolitan Opera will sing the winning song for you from the picture of the same name made by his good friend and genius, Billy Einhorn. The winner is of course Mr. Arthur M. Shaughnessy.

ARTIE *goes to the telephone. He dials once, then:* Operator, I want to call in Bel Air, Los Angeles—

BUNNY: You got the number?

ARTIE: Tattooed, baby. Tattooed. Your heart and his telephone number right on my chest like a sailor. Not you, operator. I want and fast I want in Los Angeles in Bel Air GR 2-4129 and I will not dial it because I want to speak personally to my good friend and genius, Mr. Billy Einhorn . . . E-I-N—don't you know how to spell it? The name of only Hollywood's leading director my friend and you better not give this number to any of your friends and call him up and bother him asking for screen tests.

BUNNY: When I was an operator, they made us take oaths. I had Marlon Brando's number for years and pistols couldn't've dragged it out of my head—they make you raise your right hand—

ARTIE: My number is RA 1-2276 and don't go giving that number away and I want a good connection . . . hang on, Bunny—*she takes his extended hand*—you can hear the

beepbeepbeeps—we're traveling across the country—hang
on! Ring. It's ringing. Ring.

BUNNY, *his palm and her palm forming one praying hand:*
Oh God, please—

ARTIE, *pulling away from her:* Ring. It's up. Hello? Billy? Yes,
operator, get off—that's Billy. Will you get off— *To
Bunny:* I should've called station-to-station. He picked it
right up and everything. Billy! This is Ramon Navarro! ...
No, Billy, it's Artie Shaughnessy. Artie. No, New York!
Did I wake you up! Can you hear me! Billy, hello. I got to
tell you something—first of all, I got to tell you how bad
I feel about Georgina dying—the good die young—what
can I say—and second, since you, you old bum, never
come back to your old stomping grounds—your happy
hunting grounds, I'm thinking of coming out to see you.
... I know you can fix up a tour of the studios and that'd
be great ... and you can get us hotel reservations—that's
just fine. .... But, Billy, I'm thinking I got to get away—
not just a vacation—but make a change, get a break, if
you know what I'm getting at. .... Bananas is fine. She's
right here. We were just thinking about you— NO, IT'S
NOT FINE. Billy, this sounds cruel to say but Bananas is as
dead for me as Georgina is for you. I'm in love with a
remarkable wonderful girl—yeah, she's here too—who I
should've married years ago—no, we didn't know her
years ago—I only met her two months ago—yeah....

Secretively, pulling the phone off to the corner: It's kind
of funny, a chimpanzee knocked me in the back and
kinked my back out of whack and I went to this health
club to work it out and in the steam section with all the
steam I got lost and I went into this steam room and there
was Bunny—yeah, just towels—I mean you could make a
movie out of this, it was so romantic— She couldn't see

me and she started talking about the weight she had to
take off and the food she had to give up and she started
talking about duckling with orange sauce and oysters
baked with spinach and shrimps baked in the juice of
melted sturgeon eyes which caviar comes from—well,
you know me and food and I got so excited and the
steam's getting thicker and thicker and I ripped off my
towel and kind of raped her . . . and she was quiet for a
long time and then she finally said one of the greatest
lines of all time. . . . She said, "There's a man in here." . . .
And she was in her sheet like a toga and I was all toga'd
up and I swear, Billy, we were gods and goddesses and
the steam bubbled up and swirled and it was Mount
Olympus. I'm a new man, Billy—a new man—and I got
to make a start before it's too late and I'm calling you,
crawling on my hands and knees—no, not like that, I'm
standing up straight and talking to my best buddy and
saying Can I come see you and bring Bunny and talk over
old times. . . . I'll pay my own way. I'm not asking you
for nothing. Just your friendship. I think about you so
much and I read about you in the columns and *Conduct
of Life* is playing at the Museum of Modern Art next
week and I get nervous calling you and that Doris Day
pic—well, Bunny and I fell out of our loge seats—no,
Bananas couldn't see it—she don't go out of the house
much. . . . I get nervous about calling you because, well,
you know, and I'm not asking for any Auld Lang Syne
treatment, but it must be kind of lonely with Georgina
gone and we sent five dollars in to the Damon Runyon
Cancer Fund like Walter Winchell said to do and we're
gonna send more and it must be kind of lonely and the
three of us—Bunny and you and me—could have some
laughs. What do you say? You write me and let me

know your schedule and we can come any time. But
soon. Okay, buddy? Okay? No, this is my call. I'm paying for this call so you don't have to worry—talking to
you I get all opened up. You still drinking rye? Jack
Daniels! Set out the glasses—open the bottle—no, I'll
bring the bottle—we'll see you soon. Good night, Billy.
The call is over.

   Soon, Billy. Soon. Soon. *He hangs up.*

BUNNY *dances and sings:*

> The day that the Pope came to New York
> The day that the Pope came to New York,
> It really was comical,
> The Pope wore a yarmulke
> The day that the Pope came to New York.

ARTIE, *stunned:* Did you hear me!

BUNNY: You made me sound like the Moon Coming Over
   the Mountain! So fat!

ARTIE: He said to say hello to you, Bananas.

BANANAS: Hello . . .

ARTIE, *to Bunny:* Get the copy of *Life* magazine with the story
   on his house . . .

BUNNY *gets the magazine off the top of the piano.*

BUNNY, *thrilled:* You made me sound so fat! So Kate Smith!

ARTIE, *taking the magazine and opening it:* Look at his house—
   on the highest part of all Los Angeles—

BUNNY, *devouring the pictures:* It's Bel Air! I know Bel Air!
   I mean, I don't know Bel Air, but I mean, I know Bel Air!

ARTIE *and* BUNNY *flop on the sofa.* BANANAS, *in the kitchen behind them, throws rice at them.*

BUNNY: Let's get out of here. She gives me the weeping willies.

BANANAS: Oh, no, I'm all right. I was just thinking how lucky we all are. You going off to California and me going off to the loony bin—

ARTIE, *correcting her:* It's a rest place—

BANANAS: With beautiful blue trees, huh?

ARTIE: Birds—waiting to go to Florida or California—

BANANAS: Maybe it was a flock of insane bluebirds that got committed—

ARTIE, *to Bunny:* I'm gonna take a shower. My shirt's all damp from the telephone call.

BUNNY, *putting her coat on:* Artie, I'll be at the corner of Forty-sixth Street near the cemetery by the TV repair store. . . . Hello, John the Baptist. That's who you are. John the Baptist. You called Billy and prepared the way— the way for yourself. Oh, Christ, the dinners I'm gonna cook for you. *She sings:*

> It really was comical,
> The Pope wore a yarmulke
> The day that the Pope came to New York.

She blows a kiss and exits.
ARTIE *yelps triumphantly. He comes downstage.*

ARTIE: Hello, Billy. I'm here. I got all my music. *He sings:*

> I'm here with bells on,
> Ringing out how I feel.
> I'll ring,

> I'll roar,
> I'll sing
> Encore!
> I'm here with bells on.
> Ring! Ring! Ring!

BANANAS, *very depressed:* The people downstairs . . . they'll be
pumping broomsticks on the ceiling . . .

ARTIE, *jubilant:* For once the people downstairs is Bunny! *He
sings:*

> For once the people downstairs is Bunny!

He speaks now, jumping up and down on the floor:
Whenever the conversation gets around to something you
don't like, you start ringing bells of concern for the people downstairs. For once in my life, the people downstairs
is Bunny and I am a free man! *He bangs all over the keys
of the piano.* And that's a symphony for the people upstairs!

BANANAS: There's just the roof upstairs . . .

ARTIE: Yeah, and you know roofs well. I give up six months of
my life taking care of you and one morning I wake up
and you're gone and all you got on is a nightgown and
your bare feet—the corns of your bare feet for slippers.
And it's snowing out, snowing a blizzard, and you're out
in it. Twenty-four hours you're gone and the police are up
here and long since gone and you're being broadcasted for
in thirteen states all covered with snow—and I look out
that window and I see a gray smudge in a nightgown
standing on the edge of the roof over there—in a snow-
bank and I'm praying to God and I run out of this place,
across the street. And I grab you down and you're so cold,

your nightgown cuts into me like glass breaking and I carried you back here and you didn't even catch a cold— not even a sniffle. If you had just a sniffle, I could've forgiven you. . . . You just look at me with that dead look you got right now. . . . You stay out twenty-four hours in a blizzard hopping from roof to roof without even a pair of drawers on—and *I* get the pneumonia.

BANANAS: Can I have my song?

ARTIE: You're tone-deaf. *He hits two bad notes on the piano.* Like that.

BANANAS: So I won't sing it. . . . My troubles all began a year ago—two years ago today—two days ago today? Today.

ARTIE *plays "The Anniversary Waltz."*

BANANAS: We used to have a beautiful old green Buick. The Green Latrine! . . . I'm not allowed to drive it any more . . . but when I could drive it . . . the last time I drove it, I drove into Manhattan.

ARTIE *plays "In My Merry Oldsmobile."*

BANANAS: And I drive down Broadway—to the Crossroads of the World.

ARTIE *plays "Forty-second Street."*

BANANAS: I see a scene that you wouldn't see in your wildest dreams. Forty-second Street. Broadway. Four corners. Four people. One on each corner. All waving for taxis. Cardinal Spellman. Jackie Kennedy. Bob Hope. President Johnson. All carrying suitcases. Taxi! Taxi! I stop in the middle of the street—the middle of Broadway—and I get out of my Green Latrine and yell, "Get in. I'm a gypsy. A gypsy cab. Get in. I'll take you where you want to go. Don't you all know each other? Get in! Get in!"

They keep waving for cabs. I run over to President Johnson and grab him by the arm. "Get in." And pull Jackie Kennedy into my car and John-John, who I didn't see, starts crying and Jackie hits me and I hit her and I grab Bob Hope and push Cardinal Spellman into the back seat, crying and laughing, "I'll take you where you want to go. Get in! Give me your suitcases"—and the suitcases spill open and Jackie Kennedy's wigs blow down Forty-Second Street and Cardinal Spellman hits me and Johnson screams and I hit him. I hit them all. And then the Green Latrine blew four flat tires and sinks and I run to protect the car and four cabs appear and all my friends run into four different cabs. And cars are honking at me to move.

I push the car over the bridge back to Queens. You're asleep. I turn on Johnny Carson to get my mind off and there's Cardinal Spellman and Bob Hope, whose ski-nose is still bleeding, and they tell the story of what happened to them and everybody laughs. Thirty million people watch Johnny Carson and they all laugh. At me. At me. I'm nobody. I knew all those people better than me. You. Ronnie. I know everything about them. Why can't they love me?

And then it began to snow and I went up on the roof ...

ARTIE, *after a long pause:* Come see the Pope. Pray. Miracles happen. He'll bless you. *Reader's Digest* has an article this month on how prayer answers things. Pray? Kneel down in the street? The Pope can cure you. The *Reader's Digest* don't afford to crap around.

BANANAS: My fingernails are all different lengths. Everybody'd laugh . . .

ARTIE: We used to have fun. Sometimes I miss you so much . . .

BANANAS, *smiling nervously:* If I had gloves to put on my hands . . .

ARTIE: The Pope must be landing now. I'm going to turn on the television. I want you to see him. *He turns on the television.* Here he is. He's getting off the plane. Bananas, look. Look at the screen. *He pulls her to the screen. He makes her kneel in front of it.* Oh God, help Bananas. Please God? Say a prayer, Bananas. Say, "Make me better, God . . ."

BANANAS: Make me better, God . . .

ARTIE: "So Artie can go away in peace." . . . Here's the Pope. *He speaks to the screen.* Get out of the way! Let a sick woman see! There he is! Kiss him? Kiss his hem, Bananas. He'll cure you! Kiss him.

BANANAS *leans forward to kiss the screen. She looks up and laughs at her husband.*

BANANAS: The screen is so cold . . .

ARTIE, *leaping:* Get out of the way, you goddam newsman! *He pushes Bananas aside and kisses the screen.* Help me— help me—Your Holiness . . .

While he hugs the set, BANANAS *leaves the room to go into her bedroom.*

The front door flies open. BUNNY *bursts in, flushed, bubbling. She has an enormous "I Love Paul" button on her coat.*

BUNNY: He's landed! He's landed! It's on everybody's tran-

sistors and you're still here! And the school kids!—the
Pope drives by, he sees all those school kids, he's gonna
come out for birth control today!! Churches will be selling
Holy Diaphragms with pictures of Saint Christopher and
all the saints on them. You mark my words.
To us, indicating her button: They ran out of "Welcome
Pope" buttons so I ran downstairs and got my leftover
from when the Beatles were here! I am famished. What
a day! *She goes to the icebox and downs a bottle of soda.*

BANANAS *comes out of the bedroom. She wears a coat over her
nightgown, and two different shoes, one higher than the
other, and a hat cocked on her head. She is smiling. She
is pulling on gloves.*
ARTIE *turns off the TV.*
BUNNY *gapes. Band music plays joyously in the distance.*
ARTIE *goes to Bananas and takes her arm.*

BUNNY: Now wait one minute. Miss Henshaw is going to be
mighty pissed off.
ARTIE: Just for today.
BANANAS: Hold me tight. . . .
ARTIE, *grabbing his coat:* Over the threshold . . . *They go out.*
BUNNY: Artie, are you dressed warm? Are you dressed warm?
Your music! You forgot your music! You gotta get it
blessed by the Pope!!

BANANAS *appears in the doorway and grabs the music from
Bunny.*

BANANAS *sings:*

It really was comical,
The Pope wore a yarmulke
The day that the Pope came to New York.

BUNNY: You witch! You'll be in Bellevue tonight with enough shock treatments they can plug Times Square into your ear. I didn't work for Con Edison for nothing! *She storms out after them and slams the door behind her.*

The bedroom door RONNIE *went into at the beginning of the act opens. He comes out carrying a large gift box.*
   He comes downstage and stares at us.

CURTAIN

ACT TWO

___

SCENE I

RONNIE *is standing in the same position, staring at us. Out of the pockets of his fatigues he first takes two hand grenades, then wire, then his father's alarm clock. He wires them together, setting the alarm on the clock at a special time. He puts the whole device into the gift box.*

He is very young—looks barely seventeen—his hair is cropped close all over; he is tall, skinny. He speaks with deep, suffocated religious fervor; his eyes bulge with a strange mixture of terrifying innocence and diabolism. You can't figure out whether he'd be a gargoyle on some Gothic cathedral or a skinny cherub on some altar.

RONNIE: My father tell you all about me? Pope Ronnie? Charmed life? How great I am? That's how he is with you. You should hear him with me, you'd sing a different tune pretty quick, and it wouldn't be "Where Is the Devil in Evelyn?"

He goes into his room and returns carrying a large, dusty box. He opens it and takes out an altar boy's bright red cassock and white surplice that used to fit him when he was twelve. As he puts them on, he speaks to us:

I was twelve years old and all the newspapers had headlines on my twelfth birthday that Billy was coming to town. And *Life* was doing stories on him and *Look* and the newsreels, because Billy was searching America to find the Ideal American Boy to play Huckleberry Finn. And Billy came to New York and called my father and asked him if he could stay here—Billy needed a hide-out. In Waldorf-Astorias all over the country, chambermaids would wheel in silver carts to change the sheets. And out of the sheets would hop little boys saying, "Hello, I'm Huckleberry Finn." All over the country, little boys dressed in blue jeans and straw hats would be sent to him in crates, be under the silver cover covering his dinner, in his medicine cabinet in all his hotel rooms, his suitcase— "Hello, Hello, I'm Huckleberry Finn." And he was coming here to hide out. Here—Billy coming here— I asked the nun in school who was Huckleberry Finn—

The nun in Queen of Martyrs knew. She told me. The Ideal American Boy. And coming home, all the store windows reflected me and the mirror in the tailor shop said, "Hello, Huck." The butcher shop window said, "Hello, Huck. Hello, Huckleberry Finn. All America Wants to Meet Billy and He'll Be Hiding Out in Your House." I came home—went in there—into my room and packed my bag. . . . I knew Billy would see me and take me back to California with him that very day. This room smelled of ammonia and air freshener and these slipcovers were new that day and my parents were filling up the ice-box in their brand-new clothes, filling up the icebox with food and liquor as excited as if the Pope was coming—and nervous because they hadn't seen him in a long while—Billy. They told me my new clothes were on my bed. To go get dressed. I didn't want to tell them I'd be leaving shortly to start a new life. That I'd be flying out to California with Billy on the H.M.S. *Huckleberry*. I didn't want tears from them—only trails of envy. . . . I went to my room and packed my bag and waited.

The doorbell rang. *He starts hitting two notes on the piano.* If you listen close, you can still hear the echoes of those wet kisses and handshakes and tears and backs getting hit and Hello, Billys, Hello. They talked for a long time about people from their past. And then my father called out, "Ronnie, guess who? Billy, we named him after your father. Ronnie, guess who?"

I picked up my bag and said good-bye to myself in the mirror. Came out. Billy there. Smiling.

It suddenly dawned on me. You had to do things to get parts.

I began dancing. And singing. Immediately. Things I have never done in my life—before or since. I stood on my head and skipped and whirled—*he cartwheels across the stage*—spectacular leaps in the air so I could see veins in the ceiling—ran up and down the keys of the piano and sang and began laughing and crying soft and loud to show off all my emotions. And I heard music and drums that I couldn't even keep up with. And then cut off all my emotions just like that. Instantly. And took a deep bow like the Dying Swan I saw on Ed Sullivan. *He bows deeply.* I picked up my suitcase and waited by the door.

Billy turned to my parents, whose jaws were down to about there, and Billy said, "You never told me you had a mentally retarded child."

"You never told me I had an idiot for a godchild," and I picked up my bag and went into my room and shut the door and never came out the whole time he was here.

My only triumph was he could never find a Huckleberry Finn. Another company made the picture a few years later, but it flopped.

My father thinks I'm nothing. Billy. My sergeant. They laugh at me. You laughing at me? I'm going to fool you all. By tonight, I'll be on headlines all over the world. Cover of *Time. Life.* TV specials. *He shows a picture of himself on the wall.* I hope they use this picture of me— I look better with hair— Go ahead—laugh. Because you know what I think of you? *He gives us hesitant Bronx cheers.* I'm sorry you had to hear that—pay popular prices to hear that. But I don't care. I'll show you all. I'll be too big for any of you.

The sound of a key in the door. ARTIE *is heard singing "The Day That the Pope Came to New York."*

RONNIE *exits to his room, carrying the gift box containing the bomb.*

ARTIE *runs in and begins grabbing up sheet music.*

ARTIE: Bunny says, "Arthur, I am not talking to you but I'll say it to the breeze: Arthur, get your music. 'Bring On the Girls.' Hold up your music for when the Pope His Holiness rides by."

To us: You heard these songs. They don't need blessings. I hate to get all kissyass, you know? But it can't hurt.

"Bring On the Girls." Where is it? Whenever Bunny cleans up in here you never can find anything. You should see the two girls holding each other up like two sisters and they're not even speaking which makes them even more like sisters. Wouldn't it be great if they fell in love and we all could stay . . .

A beautiful girl in a fur coat stands hesitantly in the doorway. She carries flowers and liquor in her arms. She is CORRINNA STROLLER.

CORRINNA: Mr. Shaughnessy?

ARTIE: Did I win something? Where'd I put those sweepstake tickets—I'll get them—

CORRINNA: Oh oh oh ohhhhh—it's just like Billy said. Oh God, it's like walking into a photo album. Norman Rockwell. Grandma Moses. Let me look at you. Oh, I was afraid with the Pope, you'd be out, but it's just like Billy said. You're here!

ARTIE: Billy? We talked this morning . . .

CORRINNA: Billy called me just as I was checking out and told me to stop by on my way to the airport.

ARTIE: A friend of Billy's and you stay in a hotel? Don't you know any friend of Billy's has a permanent address right here. . . . Don't tell me . . .

CORRINNA: What?

ARTIE: I know your name.

CORRINNA, *very pleased:* Oh, how could you . . .

ARTIE: You're Corrinna Stroller.

CORRINNA, *modestly:* Oh . . .

ARTIE: I knew it. I saw that one movie you made for Billy . . .

CORRINNA: That's how we met.

ARTIE: And then you retired—

CORRINNA—*a sore point:* Well ...

ARTIE: You were fantastic.

CORRINNA: Well ...

ARTIE: Why did you quit?

CORRINNA: Well ...

ARTIE: Will you sit down for a few minutes? Just let me get
my girls. If you left without seeing them. .... *He comes
down to us.* You call Billy and he sends stars. Stars! *To
Corrinna:* The icebox is yours. I'll be right back. Corrinna
Stroller! *He exits.*

CORRINNA *is alone. There is a high, loud whine. Her hands go
to her ears. The whine becomes very electronic. The sound is
almost painful. She pulls a hearing aid from each ear. The
sound suddenly stops. She reaches into her dress and removes
a receiver that the aids are wired to.*

*She sits on the couch and replaces the dead transistors
with fresh transistors. She looks up.*

CORRINNA, *to us:* Don't tell—please? I don't want them to
know I'm deaf. I don't want them to think Billy's going
around with some deaf girl. There was an accident on a
set—a set of Billy's. .... I can hear with my transistors.
She shows us a vial containing new transistors. I want
them to know me first. So please, don't tell. Please.

BUNNY *enters with Artie close behind.*

BUNNY: Where is she? Where is she? Oh—*Corrinna hastily
puts her hearing aids away*—Corrinna Stroller! Limos
in the streets. Oh, Miss Stroller, I only saw your one
movie, *Warmonger*, but it is permanently enshrined in
the Loew's of my heart. *To us:* That scene where she

blows up in the landmine—so realistic. *To Corrinna*: And then you never made another picture. What happened?

CORRINNA: I just dropped in to say hi—

BUNNY: Hi! Oh, Corrinna Stroller! *To Artie:* You know that phony Mrs. Binard in 4-C who wouldn't give you the time of day—she says, "Oh Miss Flingus, is this limo connected to you?" I'd like to put my fist through her dimple. *She takes the newspapers out of her booties. To Corrinna:* Hi, I'm Bunny, the future His. You want some snacks?

CORRINNA: I've got to catch a plane—

BUNNY: Should I send some down to the chauffeur? Oh, stay, have some snacks—

ARTIE: Are you gonna cook?

BUNNY: Just short-order snacks, while you audition . . .

ARTIE: Audition?

BUNNY: You get your ass on those tunes while the Pope's blessing is still hot on them. Artie, the Pope looked right at me! We're in solid. *To Corrinna, with a tray of celery:* Ta Ta!! That's a trumpet. Look, before we start chattering about hellos and how-are-yous and who we all are and old times and new times, bite into a celery for some quick energy and I'll get you a soda and Arthur here writes songs that could be perfect for Oscar-winning medleys and love themes of important motion-picture presentations and you should tell Billy about it. Artie being the Webster's Dictionary Definition for Mr. Shy. *Gone with the Wind. The Wizard of Oz.* That is the calibre of film that I am talking about. And His Holiness the Very Same Pope has seen these songs and given them his blessings. *She shows the sheet music to Corrinna.*

CORRINNA: I'd love to, but I have a very slight post-nasal drip.

BUNNY: Isn't she wonderful! Go on, Artie, while Mister Magic
    still shimmers!

ARTIE, *at the piano, sings:*

                Back together again,
                Back together again.

THREE NUNS *appear at the window.*

CORRINNA *sees them and screams. Her transistors fall on the*
    floor.

CORRINNA: My transistors!! *She is down on her knees, search-*
    for them.

BUNNY: Get away from here! Scat! Get away! Go! Go!

HEAD NUN: We got locked out on your roof! Please, it's fifty
    below and our fingers are icicles and our lips are the color
    of Mary—

SECOND NUN: The doorknob came right off in our hands—

ARTIE: I'm sorry, Sisters, but these are secret auditions . . .

HEAD NUN: But we missed the Pope! And we came all the way
    from Ridgewood! Let us see it on television!

ALL THREE NUNS: Please! Please! On television!

ARTIE, *opening the gate:* Oh, all right . . .

BUNNY: Don't do it, Arthur. *She sees Corrinna on the floor.*
    What's the matter, honey, did you drop something? It's
    like a regular Vatican here.

During the scene CORRINNA *will pick up her transistors at any
moment she feels she is not being observed. She keeps them in
a small vial for safety.*

The NUNS *are now inside.*

SECOND NUN: We stole Monsignor Boyle's binoculars!

HEAD NUN: We couldn't see the Pope, the crowds were so thick, so we climbed up onto your roof ...

SECOND NUN: And I put the binoculars up to my eyes and got the Pope in focus and the pressure of Him against my eyes, oh God, the binoculars flew out of my hands like a miracle in reverse ...

HEAD NUN: We'll be quiet.

LITTLE NUN, *in the kitchen:* Look! Peanut butter! They have peanut butter! *To us:* We're not allowed peanut butter!

ARTIE: Put that away!

HEAD NUN, *a sergeant:* You! Get over here.

The LITTLE NUN *obeys.* ARTIE *turns on the TV.*

SECOND NUN: Oh, color. They don't have color!

HEAD NUN: Would you have some beers? To warm us up? We will pray for you many years for your kindness today.

BANANAS, *offstage, in the hall, terrified:* Artie? Artie, are you there? Is this my home? Artie?

ARTIE: Oh God, Bananas. Bunny, get the beers, would you?

BUNNY: What do I look like?

ARTIE *runs into the hall to retrieve Bananas.*

BUNNY, *to Corrinna:* Excuse the interruption; we're not religious as such, but his heart is the Sistine Chapel. *She goes to the kitchen for beers.*

BANANAS, *entering with Artie:* I didn't know where home was. Miss Henshaw showed me. And then your fat girlfriend ran away. I had to ask directions how to get back.

BUNNY *plunks the beers on the TV set.*

SECOND NUN: Oh, imported! They don't have imported! We could've stayed back in Ridgewood and watched color and had imported, but no, she's got to see everything in the flesh—

HEAD NUN: You were the one who dropped the binoculars—

SECOND NUN: You were the one who stole them—

BANANAS: Artie, did you bring work home from the office?

ARTIE: They're nuns, Bananas, nuns.

HEAD NUN: We got locked out on the upstairs roof. Hi!

BANANAS: Hi!

ARTIE: This is Corrinna Stroller, Billy's girlfriend. Corrinna, this is Bananas.

THE NUNS: Corrinna Stroller! The movie star!

BANANAS: Hello, Billy's girlfriend. God, Billy's girlfriends always make me feel so shabby!

BUNNY, *to Corrinna:* Arthur believes in keeping family skeletons out in the open like pets. Heel, Bananas, heel!

LITTLE NUN, *running to Corrinna's side, to Corrinna:* I saw *The Sound of Music* thirty-one times. It changed my entire life.

CORRINNA: Unitarian.

ARTIE: All right now, where were we?

BUNNY: Ta Ta! The trumpet.

ARTIE, *at the piano, sings:*

> Back together again,
> Back together again . . .

HEAD NUN *screams:* There's Jackie Kennedy!!! Get me with Jackie Kennedy!!! *She puts her arm around the TV.*

The LITTLE NUN *takes out her Brownie with flash and takes a picture of the head nun posing with Jackie on TV.*

SECOND NUN: There's Mayor Lindsay! Get me with him! Mayor Lindsay dreamboat! Mayor Wagner ugh!

There is a scream from the kitchen. BANANAS *has burned herself.*

ARTIE, *running into the kitchen:* What do you think you're doing?

BANANAS: Cooking for our guests. I'm some good, Artie. I can cook.

ARTIE: What is it?

BANANAS: Hamburgers. I felt for them and I cooked them.

ARTIE: Brillo pads. You want to feed our guests Brillo pads? *To the nuns:* Sisters, please, you're going to have to go into the other room. You're upsetting my wife. *He unplugs the TV and hustles the nuns off into Ronnie's bedroom.*

SECOND NUN: Go on with what you're doing. Don't bother about us. We're nothing. We've just given our lives up praying for you. I'm going to start picking who I pray for. *She exits.*

The LITTLE NUN *crosses to the kitchen to retrieve the peanut butter.*

BUNNY: That man is a saint. That woman is a devil.

BANANAS: I'm burned.

BUNNY: Put some vinegar on it. Some salt. Take the sting out.

HEAD NUN, *coming out of the bedroom, very pleased:* There is an altar boy in here. *She exits.*

BANANAS: My son was an altar boy. He kept us in good with God. But then he grew up. He isn't an altar boy any more. *She exits into her room.*

BUNNY, *to Corrinna:* Sometimes I think the whole world has
    gone cuckoo, don't you?
CORRINNA: For two days.

The LITTLE NUN *goes into Ronnie's room as* ARTIE *comes out
and downstage.*

ARTIE, *to us:* My son Ronnie's in there! He's been picked to be
    the Pope's altar boy at Yankee Stadium—out of all the
    boys at Fort Dix! I tell you—miracles tumble down on
    this family. I don't want you to meet him yet. If his
    mother sees him, her head will go all over the wall like
    Spanish omelettes.
    To Corrinna: Are you comfortable?
BUNNY: She's adorable! And so down to earth! *She takes Cor-
    rinna's bejeweled hands.*
CORRINNA: It's five carats. It's something, isn't it?
BUNNY, *to Corrinna:* Sit right up here with Mister Maestro—
    She seats Corrinna next to Artie at the piano.
ARTIE: Where was I—
BUNNY: "Like Fido chewed them." You left off there—
ARTIE *sings as* BUNNY *dances.* BANANAS *enters and watches them.*

> ... Like Fido chewed them,
> But we're
> Back together again.
> You can say you knew us when
> We were together;
> Now we're apart,
> Thunder and lightning's
> Back in my heart,
> And that's the weather to be
> When you're back together with me.

BUNNY *claps wildly*. CORRINNA *follows suit*. BANANAS *claps slowly*.

BUNNY: Encore! Encore!

ARTIE, *happy now*: What should I play next?

BUNNY: Oh God, how do you pick a branch from a whole Redwood Forest?

BANANAS, *licking her hand*: "I Love You So I Keep Dreaming."

BUNNY *picks up the phone, but doesn't dial*: Come and get her!

BANANAS: Play "I Love You So I Keep Dreaming."

ARTIE, *pleased*: You really remember that?

BANANAS: How could I forget it . . .

BUNNY: I'm not used to being Queen of the Outsiders. What song is this?

ARTIE: I almost forgot it. It must have been like Number One that I ever wrote. The one that showed me I should go on.

BUNNY: Well, let me hear it.

ARTIE: You really surprise me, Bananas. Sometimes I miss you so much . . .

BUNNY, *warning*: Arthur, I still haven't forgiven you for this morning.

ARTIE *sings*:

> I love you so I keep dreaming
> Of all the lovely times we shared . . .

BUNNY: Heaven. That is unadulterated heaven.

BANANAS, *interrupting*: Now play "White Christmas"?

BUNNY: Shocks for sure.

BANANAS, *banging the keys of the piano*: Play "White Christmas"?

ARTIE, *to Corrinna*: She's . . . not feeling too . . . hot . . .

BUNNY, *to Corrinna*: In case you haven't noticed . . .

ARTIE: She keeps crawling under the weather . . . *He plays a run on the piano.*

BANANAS: "White Christmas"???????

ARTIE *groans, then plays and sings "White Christmas."*

BUNNY, *to Corrinna:* It really burns me up all these years The Telephone Hour doing salutes to fakers like Richard Rodgers. Just listen to that. Blaaaagh.

ARTIE *stops playing.*

BANANAS: Don't you hear it?
ARTIE *plays and sings slowly:*

> I'm dreaming of a . . .
> I love you so I . . .

They are the same tune.

ARTIE: Oh God. Oh God.
BANANAS *sings desperately:*

> I love you so I keep dreaming—

Are you tone deaf? Can't you hear it? *She bangs the keys on the piano.*

ARTIE *slams the lid shut on her hand. She yells and licks her fingers to get the pain off them.*

ARTIE: Oh, you have had it, Little Missy. All these years you knew that and made me play it. She's always trying to do that, Corrinna. Always trying to embarrass me. You have had it, Little Missy. Did Shakespeare ever write one original plot? You tell me that?

He drags Bananas down to the edge of the stage.

To us: In front of all of you, I am sorry. But you are looking at someone who has had it.

BANANAS: I am just saying your song sounds an awful lot like "White—

ARTIE: Then they can sing my song in the summertime. *He pushes her away and picks up the phone.*

BANANAS: Who are you calling?

BUNNY: Do it, Arthur.

BANANAS, *terrified:* Artie, who are you calling??????

BUNNY: Do you have a little suitcase? I'll start you packing.

BANANAS, *to Corrinna:* Billy's friend? Help me? Billy wouldn't want them to do this. Not to me. He'd be mad. *Whispering desperately, grabbing Corrinna's hands:* Help me? Bluebirds. He'll tell you all about it. Me walking on the roof. Can't you say anything? You want bribes? Here— take these flowers. They're for you. Take this liquor. For you. *She is hysterical.*

BUNNY *pulls her away and slaps her.*

BANANAS: I'll be quiet. I'll take my pills. *She reaches for the vial containing Corrinna's transistors and swallows them.*

CORRINNA, *to us:* My transistors!

ARTIE, *on the telephone:* This is Mr. Shaughnessy. Arthur M. ... I was out there last week and talked about my wife.

BANANAS: That's why my ears were burning ...

ARTIE: I forgot which doctor I talked to.

BANANAS: He had a mustache.

ARTIE: He had a mustache. *To his wife:* Thank you. *Into the*

phone: Doctor? Hello? That's right, Doctor, could you
come and ... all that we talked about. The room over the
garage is fine. Yes, Doctor. Now. Today. ... Really? That
soon? She'll be all ready. ... *He hangs up the phone.*

BUNNY: Arthur, give me your hand. Like I said, today's my
wedding day. I wanted something white at my throat.
Look, downstairs in a pink cookie jar, I got a thousand
dollars saved up and we are flying out to California with
Corrinna. As soon as Bananas here is carted off, we'll step
off that plane and Billy and you and I and Corrinna here
will eat and dance and drink and love until the middle of
the next full moon. *To Bananas:* Bananas, honey, it's not
just a hospital. They got dances. *To Corrinna:* Corrinna,
I'll be right back with my suitcase. *To Artie:* Artie, start
packing. All my life I been treated like an old shoe. You
turned me into a glass slipper. *She sings:*

> I'm here with bells on.
> Ring! Ring! Ring! Ring! Ring!

She exits.

ARTIE: I'm sorry. I'm sorry.

BANANAS *runs into her bedroom.*
CORRINNA *edges toward the front door.*

ARTIE: Well, Corrinna, now you know everything. Dirty laun-
dry out in the open. I'll be different out West. I'm great
at a party. I never took a plane trip before. I guess that's
why my stomach is all queasied up. ... Hey, I'd better
start packing. ... *He exits.*

CORRINNA *heads for the door. The* NUNS *enter.*

HEAD NUN: Miss Stroller! Miss Stroller! He told us all about Hollywood and Billy and Huckleberry Finn—

SECOND NUN: You tell Billy he ought to be ashamed treating a boy like that—

LITTLE NUN, *with paper and pen:* Miss Stroller, may I have your autograph?

CORRINNA: Sisters, pray for me? Pray my ears come out all right. I'm leaving for Australia—

THE NUNS: Australia?!?

CORRINNA: For a very major ear operation and I need all the prayers I can get. *To us:* South Africa's where they do the heart work, but Australia's the place for ears. So pray for me. Pray my operation's a success.

ARTIE *enters with his suitcase half-packed.*

ARTIE: Australia?

CORRINNA: I'm so glad I made a new friend my last day in America.

THE NUNS: She's going to Australia!

CORRINNA: Perhaps you'll bring me luck.

ARTIE: Your last day in America? Sisters, please.

CORRINNA: I'll be Mrs. Einhorn the next time you see me. . . . Billy and I are off to Australia tomorrow for two fabulous years. Billy's making a new film that is an absolute breakthrough for him—*Kangaroo*—and you must—all of you—come to California.

THE NUNS: *Kangaroo*! California!

CORRINNA: And we'll be back in two years.

ARTIE: But we're coming with you today . . .

The NUNS *are praying for Corrinna.*

LITTLE NUN: Our Father, Who art in heaven . . .

SECOND NUN: You shut up. I want to pray for her. Our Father—

HEAD NUN *blows a whistle:* I'll pray for her. *She sings:*

Ave Maria—

The THREE NUNS *sing "Ave Maria."*

RONNIE *enters wearing his army overcoat over the altar boy's cassock and carrying the box with the bomb. He speaks over the singing.*

RONNIE: Pop! Pop! I'm going!

ARTIE: Ronnie! Corrinna, this is the boy. *To us:* He's been down to Fort Dix studying to be a general—

RONNIE: Pop, I'm going to blow up the Pope.

ARTIE: See how nice you look with your hair all cut—

The NUNS *have finished singing "Ave Maria" and take flash pictures of themselves posing with Corrinna.*

RONNIE: Pop, I'm going to blow up the Pope and when *Time* interviews me tonight, I won't even mention you. I'll say I was an orphan.

ARTIE: Ronnie, why didn't you write and let me know you were coming home? I might've been in California— It's great to see you—

CORRINNA *runs to the front door, then stops:* Oh, wait a minute. The Pope's Mass at Yankee Stadium! I have two tickets for the Pope's Mass at Yankee Stadium! Would anybody like them?

The NUNS *and* RONNIE *rush Corrinna for the tickets, forcing her back against the door.* RONNIE *wins the tickets and comes downstage to retrieve his gift-wrapped bomb. When he turns around to leave, the* THREE NUNS *are advancing threateningly on him. They will not let him pass. They lunge at him. He runs into the bedroom for protection.*

ARTIE, *at the front door:* Miss Stroller, two years? Let's get this Australia part straight. Two years?

An M.P. *steps between Artie and Corrinna and marches into the room. The* M.P. *searches the room.*

ARTIE: Who are you? What are you doing here? Can I help you?
CORRINNA: Oh! This must be Ronnie! The son in the Army! I can't *wait* to hear all about you! *She embraces the* M.P.

The M.P. *hears the noises and fighting from Ronnie's room and runs in there.*

CORRINNA, *to Artie:* He looks just like you!
ARTIE, *following the* M.P.*:* You can't barge into a house like this—where are you going?

The LITTLE NUN *runs out of the bedroom, triumphantly waving the tickets, almost knocking Artie over.*

LITTLE NUN: I got 'em! I got 'em!

RONNIE *runs out after her. The other* TWO NUNS *run after him. The* M.P. *runs after them.* RONNIE *runs into the kitchen after the* LITTLE NUN, *who leaps over the couch.* RONNIE *leaps after her. He lands on top of her. He grabs the tickets.*

HEAD NUN, *to the* M.P.: Make him give us back our tickets.

M.P. *takes a deep breath and then:* Ronald-V.-Shaughnessy.-You-are-under-arrest-for-being-absent-without-leave.-You-have-the-right-to-remain-silent.-I-must-warn-you-that-any-thing-you-say-may-be-used-against-you-in-a-military-court-of-law.-You-have-the-right-to-counsel.-Do-you-wish-to-call-counsel?

RONNIE *attempts escape. The* HEAD NUN *bears down on him.*

HEAD NUN: That altar boy stole our tickets!

SECOND NUN: Make him give them back to us!

RONNIE *throws the tickets down. The* HEAD NUN *grabs them.*

HEAD NUN, *to the little nun:* You! Back to Ridgewood! Yahoo!
    She exits.

SECOND NUN, *to Corrinna:* Good luck with your ear operation.
    She exits.

CORRINNA: This is an invitation—come to California.

RONNIE, *tossing the bomb to Corrinna:* From me to Billy—

CORRINNA: Oh, how sweet. I can't wait to open it. Hold the
    elevator!! *She runs out.*

ARTIE, *to the* M.P., *who is struggling with Ronnie:* Hey, what
    are you doing to my boy?!?

A MAN *dressed in medical whites enters.*

WHITE MAN: I got a radio message to pick up a Mrs. Arthur
    M. Shaughnessy.

ARTIE: Bananas! *He runs to her bedroom.*

BUNNY, *dancing in through the front door, beaming and*

dressed like a million bucks: Ta Ta! Announcing Mrs.
Arthur M. Shaughnessy!
WHITE MAN: That's the name. Come along.
BUNNY, *to us, sings:*

> I'm here with bells on,
> Ringing out how I feel . . .

The WHITE MAN *slips the strait jacket on Bunny. She struggles.
He drags her out. She's fighting wildly.* ARTIE *returns.*

ARTIE: Wait. Stop.

RONNIE *pulls him from the door as there is a terrible explosion.
Pictures fly off the wall. Smoke pours in from the hall.*

BUNNY, *entering through the smoke:* Artie? Where's Corrinna? Where's Corrinna?
ARTIE: Corrinna?

ARTIE *runs out into the hall with* BUNNY.
The lights dim as RONNIE *and the* M.P. *grapple in slow motion,
the* LITTLE NUN *trying to pull the* M.P. *off Ronnie.*
BANANAS *comes downstage into the light. An unattached
vacuum hose is wrapped around her shoulders. She cleans the
floor with the metallic end of the hose. She smiles at us.*

BANANAS, *to us:* My house is a mess. . . . Let me straighten up.
. . . I can do that. . . . I'm a housewife. . . . I'm good for
something. . . . *She sings as she vacuums:*

> I love you so I keep dream . . .

She closes her eyes. Artie, you could salvage that song. You really could.

CURTAIN

S C E N E   2

In the darkness after the curtain we hear the POPE *from Yankee Stadium. He gives his speech in heavily accented English. An announcer provides simultaneous translation in unaccented English.*

VOICE OF THE POPE: We feel, too, that the entire American people is here present with its noblest and most characteristic traits: a people basing its conception of life on spiritual values, on a religious sense, on freedom, on loyalty, on work, on the respect of duty, on family affection, on generosity and courage—

The curtain goes up.

It is later that night, and the only illumination in the room is the light from the television.

The house is vaguely picked up but not repaired, and everything is askew: neat—things are picked up off the floor, for instance—but lampshades are just tilted enough, pictures on the wall just slanted enough, and we see that everything that had been on the floor—the clothes, the suitcases—has been jammed into corners.

ARTIE *is watching the television.*

Another person is sitting in the easy chair in front of the TV.

—safeguarding the American spirit from those dangers which prosperity itself can entail and which the materialism of our day can make even more menacing. . . . From its brief but heroic history, this young and flourishing country can derive lofty and convincing examples to encourage us all in its future progress.

From the easy chair, we hear sobbing. The deep sobbing of a man.
ARTIE *clicks off the television and clicks on the lights. He has put a coat and tie over his green park clothes. He's very uncomfortable and is trying to be very cheery. The* MAN *in the chair keeps sobbing.*

ARTIE: I'm glad he said that. That Pope up at Yankee Stadium —some guy. Boy, isn't that Pope some guy. You ever met him in your travels? . . . You watch. That gang war in Vietnam—over tomorrow . . .
Brightly: People always talking about a certain part of the anatomy of a turkey like every Thanksgiving you say give me the Pope's nose. But that Pope is a handsome guy. Not as good-looking as you and me, but clean. Businesslike.
To us: This is the one. The only. You guessed it: this is Billy. He got here just before the eleven o'clock news. He had to identify Corrinna's body, so he's a little upset. You forgive him, okay?
Billy, come on—don't take it so hard. . . . You want to take off your shoes? . . . You want to get comfortable? . . . You want a beer? . . . *He sits at the piano and plays and sings:*

> If there's a broken heart
> For every light on Broadway,
> Screw in another bulb . . .

You like that? . . . Look, Billy, I'm sorry as hell we had to get together this way. . . . Look at it this way. It was quick. No pain. Pain is awful, but she was one of the luckies, Bill. She just went. And the apartment is all insured. They'll give us a new elevator and everything.

BILLY: The one thing she wanted was . . .

ARTIE: Come on, boy. Together. Cry, cry, get it all out.

BILLY: She wanted her footprints in Grauman's Chinese. I'm going to have her shoes set in wet cement. A ceremony. A tribute. God knows she'd hate it.

ARTIE: Hate it?

BILLY: Ahh, ever since the ears went, she stopped having the push, like she couldn't hear her different drummer any more, drumming up all that push to get her to the top. She just stopped. *He cries. Deep sobs.*

ARTIE, *uncomfortable:* She could've been one of the big ones. A lady Biggie. Boy. Stardust. Handfuls of it. All over her. Come on, boy . . . easy . . . easy . . . *Impatient:* Bill, that's enough.

BILLY: Do you have any tea bags?

ARTIE: You want a drink? Got the bourbon here—the Jack Daniels—

BILLY: No. Tea bags. Two. One for each eye.

ARTIE, *puzzled:* Coming right up. . . . *He goes into the kitchen and opens the cabinets.*

BILLY: Could you wet them? My future is all ashes, Artie. In the morning, I'll fly back with Corrinna's body, fly back to L.A. and stay there. I can't work. Not for a long, long

time, if ever again. I was supposed to go to Australia, but
no . . . all ashes. . . . *He puts one wet tea bag over each eye.*
God, it's good to see you again, Artie.

ARTIE: Billy, you can't! You owe it—golly, Billy, the world—
Bunny and me—we fell out of our loge seats—I'd be
crazy if it wasn't for the laughs, for the romance you
bring. You can't let this death stand in the way. Look
what's happened to your old buddy. I've become this
Dreaming Boy. I make all these Fatimas out of the future.
Lourdes and Fatima. All these shrines out of the future
and I keep crawling to them. Don't let that happen to
you. Health. Health. You should make a musical. Listen
to this. *He goes to the piano and plays and sings:*

> Back together again,
> Back together again . . .

BANANAS *appears in the bedroom doorway dressed in clothes
that must have been very stylish and elegant ten years earlier.*

BILLY *starts:* Georgina!!

ARTIE *stops playing.*

BANANAS: No, Billy . . .

BILLY *stands up:* Oh God—for a minute I thought it was . . .

ARTIE: Don't she look terrific . . .

BILLY: Let me look at you. Turn around. *She does.* Jesus,
didn't Georgina have good taste.

BANANAS, *turning:* I used to read *Vogue* on the newsstands to
see what I'd be wearing in three years.

BILLY: Georgina took that dress right off her back and gave it
to you. What a woman *she* was . . .

BILLY *is crying again.*

BANANAS: I put it on to make you happy, Billy.

ARTIE: Easy, Billy, easy . . .

BANANAS: It's a shame it's 1965. I'm like the best-dressed woman of 1954.

BILLY, *starting to laugh and cheer up:* You got the best of them all, Artie. Hello, Bananas!

BANANAS: Sometimes I curse you for giving me that name, Billy.

BILLY: A little Italian girl. What else was I going to call her?

The LITTLE NUN *rushes in from the bedroom, her habit wet.*

LITTLE NUN: Mr. Shaughnessy! Quick—the bathtub—the shower—the hot water is steaming—running over—I can't turn it—there's nothing to turn—

ARTIE *runs into the bedroom. The* LITTLE NUN *looks at Billy.* BILLY *smiles at her. The* LITTLE NUN *runs into the bedroom.* BANANAS *show him a spigot.*

BANANAS: I did it to burn her.

BILLY: Burn who?

BANANAS: Burn her downstairs. Have the hot water run through the ceiling and give her blisters. He won't like her so much when she's covered with blisters. Hot water can do that. It's one of the nicest properties of hot water.

BILLY: Burn who???

BANANAS: Kate Smith!! *She holds the spigot behind her back.*

ARTIE, *running in from the bedroom to the kitchen:* Wrench. Wrench. Screwdriver. *He rattles through drawers. Brightly, to Billy:* God, don't seem possible. Twenty years ago. All started right on this block. Didn't we have some times? The Rainbow Room. Leon and Eddie's. I got the pictures right here.

The pictures are framed on the wall by the front door. BILLY *comes up to them.*

BILLY: Leon and Eddie's!

ARTIE, *indicating another picture:* The Village Barn.

BANANAS: The Village Barn. God, I loved the Village Barn.

ARTIE: It's closed, Bananas. Finished. Like you.

LITTLE NUN: Mr. Shaughnessy—please?

ARTIE *runs into the bedroom.*

LITTLE NUN: Mr. Einhorn?

BILLY: Hello?

LITTLE NUN: I was an usher before I went in and your name always meant quality. *She runs into the bedroom.*

BILLY: Why— Thank you . . .

BANANAS: Help me, Billy? They're coming again to make me leave. Let me stay here? They'll listen to you. You see, they give me pills so I won't feel anything. Now I don't mind not feeling anything so long as I can remember feeling. You see? And this apartment, you see, here, right here, I stand in this corner and I remember laughing so hard. Doubled up. At something Ronnie did. Artie said. And I stand over here where I used to iron. When I could iron, I'd iron right here, and even then, the buttons, say, on button-down shirts could make me sob, cry . . . and that window, I'd stand right here and mix me a rye-and-ginger pick-me-up and watch the lights go on in the Empire State Building and feel so tender . . . unprotected.

... I don't mind not feeling so long as I can be in a place I remember feeling. You get me? You get me? Don't look at me dead. I'm no Georgina. I'm no Corrinna. Help me? Help Ronnie?

BILLY: Ronnie's in jail.

BANANAS: I don't mind the bars. But he can't take them. He's not strong like his mom. Come closer to me? Don't let them hear. *She strokes his eyebrows.* Oh, you kept your mustache. Nothing's changed. *She sings:*

Should auld acquaintance be forgot ...

ARTIE *comes out of the bedroom, soaking wet:* Those are eyebrows, Bananas. Eyebrows. Come on, where is it? *He reaches behind Bananas's back and pulls the silver faucet handle from her clenched fist.* Billy, you see the wall I'm climbing? *He goes back into the bedroom with it.*

The LITTLE NUN *looks out into the living room.*

LITTLE NUN, *to Billy:* We never got introduced.

BILLY: Do I know you?

BANANAS *goes into the corner by the window.*

LITTLE NUN, *coming into the room:* No, but my two friends died with your friend today.

BILLY: I'm very sorry for you.

LITTLE NUN: No, it's all right. All they ever wanted to do was die and go to heaven and meet Jesus. The convent was very depressing. Pray a while. Scream a while. Well, they got their wish, so I'm happy.

BILLY: If your friends died with my friend, then that makes

us—oh God! Bananas! That makes us all friends! You
friends and me friends and we're all friends!

BANANAS: Help Ronnie. Help him. *She hands Billy the phone.*

BILLY, *on the phone:* Operator—my friend the operator—get
me person-to-person my friend General Buckley Revere
in the Pentagon—202 LIncoln 5-5600.

ARTIE, *coming out of the bedroom:* No, Billy . . . no favors for
Ronnie. The kid went AWOL. M.P.'s dragging him out
of the house. You think I like that? *To Bananas:* That
kid's your kid, Bananas. You got the crazy monopoly on
all the screwball chromosomes in that kid.

BILLY: Buck? Bill.

ARTIE, *to Bananas:* Let him learn responsibility. Let him learn
to be a man.

BILLY: Buck, just one favor: my godchild, Ron Shaughnessy.
He's in the brig at Fort Dix. He wanted to see the Pope.

ARTIE, *to Bananas:* Billy and me served our country. You think
Billy could call up generals like that if he wasn't a veteran!
To us: I feel I got to apologize for the kid. . . . I tried to
give him good strong things . . .

BILLY: Buck, has the Army lost such heart that it won't let a
simple soldier get a glimpse of His Holiness . . .

The front door opens. BUNNY *enters. She looks swell and great
and all the Webster Dictionary synonyms for terrific. She's all
exclamation points: pink and white!!! She carries an open umbrella and a steaming casserole in her potholder-covered
hands.*

BUNNY: Arthur, are you aware *The Rains of Ranchipur* are
currently appearing on my ceiling?

ARTIE: Ssshhhhhhh. . . . *Indicating her pot:* Is that the veal and
oranges?

BUNNY: That's right, Arthur. I'm downstairs making veal and oranges and what do I get from you? Boiling drips.

ARTIE: That's Billy. . . . Billy's here. *He takes the umbrella from her.*

BUNNY: Billy Einhorn here? And you didn't call me? Oh, Mr. Einhorn. *She steps into the room. She is beaming. She poses.* And that's why the word Voilà was invented. Excuse my rudeness. Hi, Artie. Hi, Bananas.

BILLY, *on the phone:* Thank you, Buck. Yes, Yes, Terrific, Great. Talk to you tomorrow. Love ya. Thank you. *He hangs up.* Ronnie'll be all right. Buck will have him stationed in Rome with NATO. He'll do two weeks in the brig just to clear the records. . . .

ARTIE: Then off to Rome? Won't that be interesting. And educational. Thank you, Billy. Thank you.

BILLY: Ronnie's lucky. Buck said everybody at Dix is skedded for Vietnam.

BUNNY: I wouldn't mind that. I love Chinese food.

ARTIE: That's the little girl from the steambath . . .

BILLY *notices Bunny. They laugh.*

BUNNY: Hi! I'm Bunny from right down below.

BILLY *kisses her hand.*

BUNNY: Oohhhh. . . . Artie, perhaps our grief-stricken visitor from Movieland would join us in a Snack à la Petite.

BILLY: No, no.

ARTIE: Come on, Bill.

BUNNY: Flying in on such short notice you must have all the starving people of Armenia in your tumtum, begging, "Feed me, feed me."

BILLY: Just a bite would be—

BANANAS *comes down to us with Artie's scrapbook*: What they do is they make a scrapbook of all the things she can cook, then they paste them in the book—veal parmagina, eggplant meringue . . .

ARTIE *grabs it from her.*

BANANAS: Eughh . . .

ARTIE, *to Billy:* We make a scrapbook of all the things Bunny can cook, you see, then we paste them in the book.

BUNNY *serves.* ARTIE *takes a deep breath. He tastes.*

ARTIE, *to us:* I wish I had spoons enough for all of you.

They eat.

BUNNY: Mr. Einhorn, I met your friend today before Hiroshima Mon Amour happened out there and all I got to say is I hope when I go I got two Sisters of Charity with me. I don't know your persuasion God-wise, but your friend Corrinna, whether she likes it or not, is right up there in heaven tonight.

BILLY: Artie, you were right. We are what our women make us. Corrinna: how easily deaf becomes dead. It was her sickness that held us together. Health. Health. You were always healthy. You married a wonderful little Italian girl. You have a son. Where am I?

BUNNY: Deaf starlets. That's no life.

BILLY: So how come she's dead? Who blew her up?

BANANAS: It was on the eleven o'clock news.

BUNNY: Crying and explanations won't bring her back. Mr.

Einhorn, if it took all this to get you here, I kiss the calendar for today. Grief puts erasers in my ears. My world is kept a beautiful place. Artie . . . I feel a song coming on.

ARTIE: How about a lovely tune, Bill, to go with that food. *He goes to the piano and plays.*

BUNNY *opens the umbrella and does a dance with it, as she sings:*

> Where is the devil in Evelyn?
> What's it doing in Angela's eyes?
> Evelyn is heavenly,
> Angela's in a devil's disguise.
> I know about the sin in Cynthia
> And the hell in Helen of Troy,
> But where is the devil in Evelyn?
> What's it doing in Angela's eyes?
> Oh boy!
> What's it doing in Angela's eyes?

BILLY: My God!

ARTIE, *up from the piano:* What!

BILLY: Suddenly!

BANANAS: Was it the veal?

BILLY: I see future tenses! I see I can go on! Health! I have an extra ticket. Corrinna's ticket. For Australia.

ARTIE: God, Billy, I'd love to. I have all my music . . . ARTIE *races to Billy.*

BILLY, *coming to Bunny:* Cook for me a while? Stay with me a while? In two hours a plane leaves from Kennedy and on to a whole new world. Los Angeles. We drop off Corrinna's body. Then on to Hawaii. Samoa. Nonstop to Melbourne. Someone who listens. That's what I need.

BUNNY: But my whole life is here ...

BILLY: Chekhov was right. Work. Work. That's the only answer. All aboard??????

BUNNY: My my my my my my my ...

ARTIE: Are you out of your head? Leaving in two hours? It takes about six months to get shots and passports—

BUNNY: Luckily two years ago I got shots and a passport in case I got lucky with a raffle ticket to Paree. *To us:* I'm in raffles all over the place.

ARTIE: Bunny—

BUNNY: Leave me alone, Arthur. I have to think. I don't know what to say. It's all so sudden.

The LITTLE NUN *comes out of the bedroom. She is in civvies. As a matter of fact, she has on one of Georgina's dresses, off the shoulder, all covered with artificial cherries. It is too big for her. She carries her wet habit.*

LITTLE NUN: I was catching a cold so I put on one of your dresses, Mrs. Shaughnessy. I have to go now. I want to thank you for the loveliest day I've ever had. You people are so lucky. You have so much. *She is near tears.* And your son is so cute. Maybe when I take my final vows I can cross my fingers and they won't count.

BILLY: How would you like to stay here?

ARTIE: Stay here?

BILLY: There'll be an empty apartment right down below and you could come up and take care of Bananas. *He takes out his wallet and gives a number of hundred-dollar bills to the little nun.* How's this for a few months' salary?

ARTIE: What's all that money?

BILLY: Artie, don't send Bananas away. Love. That's all she needs.

BANANAS: It is? *The telephone rings. She answers it:* Yes? Yes? *To Artie, who is on his knees, trying to reason with Bunny:* It's the Zoo.

ARTIE: Tell them I'll call—what are they calling this late for?

BANANAS: The animals are all giving birth! Everything's having a baby. The leopards and the raccoons and the gorillas and the panthers and the . . .

ARTIE, *taking the phone:* Who is this? Al? Look, this is what you have to do. Heat the water. Lock the male elephants out. They get testy. The leopardess tends to eat her children. Watch her careful . . .

As he talks on the phone so we can't hear him, BUNNY *comes downstage and talks to us.*

BUNNY: The Pope saw my wish today. He looked me right in the eye and he winked. Hey! Smell—the bread is starting again and there's miracles in the air! The Pope is flying back through the nighttime sky and all the planets fall back into place and Orion the Hunter relaxes his bow . . . and the gang war in Vietnam will be over and all those crippled people can now stand up and walk back to Toledo. And, Billy, in front of all these people, I vow to you I'll be the best housekeeper money can buy . . . and I'll cook for you and clean and, who knows, maybe there'll be a development. . . . And, Bananas, honey, when I get to California, I'll send you some of my clothes. I'll keep up Georgina's traditions. Sister, here are the keys to my apartment downstairs. You can write a book, "I Jump Over the Wall," and, Billy, you could film it.

ARTIE, *on the phone:* Yes! I'll be right down. I'll be right on the subway. Yes. *He hangs up.* I . . . have to go to work.

. . . Billy? Bun? Would you like to come? See life starting? It's beautiful.

BUNNY, *in the kitchen:* Bananas, honey, could I have this cop-
per pot? I've always had my eye on this pot.

BANANAS: Take it.

ARTIE: Listen, Bill.

BUNNY: Well, I'm packed.

ARTIE: I write songs, Bill. *He starts playing and singing "Back
Together Again."*

BANANAS, *to Billy, who is on his way out:* Thank you, Billy.

BILLY, *coming back and sitting alongside Artie:* Artie, can I
tell you a secret?

ARTIE *stops playing.*

BILLY: Do you know who I make my pictures for? Money?
No. Prestige? No. I make them for you.

ARTIE: Me?

BILLY: I sit on the set and before every scene I say, "Would
this make Artie laugh? Would this make Artie cry?"

ARTIE: I could come on the set and tell you personal . . .

BILLY: Oh no, Artie. If I ever thought you and Bananas weren't
here in Sunnyside, seeing my work, loving my work, I
could never work again. You're my touch with reality.
He goes to Bananas. Bananas, do you know what the
greatest talent in the world is? To be an audience. Anybody can create. But to be an audience . . . be an audience . . .

ARTIE *runs back to the piano. He sings desperately:*

I'm looking for something,
I've searched everywhere . . .

BUNNY: Artie, I mean this in the best possible sense: You've
    been a wonderful neighbor.
BILLY, *to Artie:* I just saved your life.

BILLY *takes Bunny's hand and leads her out.*
ARTIE *plays "Where Is the Devil in Evelyn?" hysterically, then
    runs out after them, carrying his sheet music.*

ARTIE, *shouting:* Bill! Bill! I'm too old to be a young talent!!!

The LITTLE NUN *comes downstage, her hands filled with
money.*

LITTLE NUN, *to us:* Life is this orchard and we walk beneath it
    and apples and grapes and cherries and mangoes all tum-
    ble down on us. Ask and you shall receive. I didn't even
    ask and look how much I have. Thank you. Thank you
    all.
    She kisses the television. A shrine . . . I wanted to be a
    Bride of Christ but I guess now I'm a young divorcee.
    I'll go downstairs and call up the convent. Good-bye.
    Thank you. *She wrings out her wet habit, then throws it
    up in the air and runs out.*

BANANAS *turns off all the lights in the room.* ARTIE *returns.
He stands in the doorway.* BANANAS *sits on the edge of the
armchair. She is serene and peaceful and beautiful in the dim
light.* ARTIE *comes into the room slowly. He lets his music
slip to the floor.*

BANANAS: I don't blame you for that lady, Artie. I really don't.
    But I'm going to be good to you now. Cooking. I didn't
    know you liked cooking. All these years and I didn't

know you liked cooking. See, you can live with a person . . . Oh God, Artie, it's like we're finally alone for the first time in our life. Like it's taken us eighteen years to get from the church to the hotel room and we're finally alone. I promise you I'll be different. I promise you . . .

He smiles at her, hopefully.

Hello, Artie.

She sits on her haunches like a little dog smiling for food. She sings:

> Back together again,
> Back together again.
> Since we split up
> The skies we lit up
> Looked all bit up
> Like Fido chewed them,
> But they're
> Back together again.
> You can say you knew us when . . .

She barks. She sits up, begging, her hands tucked under her chin. She rubs her face into Artie's legs. He pats her head. She is thrilled. He kneels down in front of her. He touches her face. She beams. She licks his hand. He kisses her. He strokes her throat. He looks away. He holds her. He kisses her fully. She kisses him. He leans into her. As his hands go softly on her throat, she looks up at him with a beautiful smile as if she had always been waiting for this. He kisses her temples, her cheeks. His hands tighten around her throat. Their bodies blend as he moves on top of her. She smiles radiantly at him. He squeezes the breath out of her throat. She falls.

Soft piano music plays.

The stage begins to change. Blue leaves begin to filter all over the room until it looks like ARTIE *is standing in a forest of leaves that are blue. A blue spotlight appears downstage and he steps into it. He is very happy and smiles at us.*

ARTIE: Hello. My name is Artie Shaughnessy and I'd like to thank you for that blue spot and to sing you some songs from the pen of. *He sings:*

> I'm here with bells on,
> Ringing out how I feel.
> I'll ring,
> I'll roar,
> I'll sing
> Encore!
> I'm here with bells on.
> Ring! Ring! Ring!

The stage is filled with blue leaves.

CURTAIN

BOSOMS
AND
NEGLECT

———

FOR ADELE

CHARACTERS

Henny
Scooper
Deirdre

Bosoms and Neglect, directed by Mel Shapiro, was presented by Bernard Gersten and John Wulp in association with Marc Howard at the Longacre Theatre, in New York City, on May 3, 1979. An initial engagement at the Goodman Theatre, Chicago, Illinois (Gregory Mosher, artistic director), opened March 1, 1979.

CAST

HENNY	*Kate Reid*
SCOOPER	*Paul Rudd*
DEIRDRE	*Marian Mercer*

The scenery was by John Wulp. Costumes were by Willa Kim. The lighting was by Jennifer Tipton.

In a production of *Bosoms and Neglect*, directed by Larry Arrick, with a cast including Richard Kavanaugh, Anne Meara and April Shawhan, presented at the Perry Street Theatre through the auspices of the New York Theater Workshop, 26 March – 20 April 1986, a number of additional lines and scenes were written into the play.

The text reproduced here incorporates those changes.

A production of the same play, with Eve Pearce, Campbell Graham and Deborah Weston, directed by Daniel Banks, was produced by Theatro Technis, London, 7–29 February 1992.

PROLOGUE

———

Henny's apartment in Queens.
Summer storm. Rain. Thunder.
HENNY *sings in a raucous voice a pop tune along the lines of*
"Caught Between Two Lovers." Her voice comes from behind
the window curtain.
SCOOPER *lets himself into the apartment. He is forty, fit, trim.*

SCOOPER: I found a doctor who'll make house calls. *He passes*
   through the room without taking off his soaking wet rain-
   coat and hat. The singing continues. Offstage: Talk about
   Mission Impossible. I'm sorry I'm late. He'll be here in
   about fifteen minutes.
HENNY, *behind the curtain:* Oh God. Oh God. Oh God.

SCOOPER *comes back into the room holding an empty washed*
mayonnaise jar. He pulls back the window curtain. HENNY
stands there, her fingers in her ears, still singing. She is old.
She is blind. Her spirit is strong.

SCOOPER: This house-call doctor wants you to fill up a jar so he can take it to the lab. I have to bring it up to the pharmacy on Eighty-second Street. So can you fill this up?

HENNY: I don't have to go.

SCOOPER: *Now* you don't have to go.

HENNY: I don't have any cystitis.

SCOOPER: Don't go screaming and crying and shaking so hard. He can't get a look at you if you're screaming and crying and shaking so hard. I told him it burns when you pee. I told him it's probably cystitis. Don't close your ears and hum. Listen to me. Valerie said it sounds like cystitis. It's a ladies' sickness. Valerie said if it burns when she pees, it sounds like cystitis to me. I told the doctor it was probably cystitis. That's what Valerie says.

HENNY: Valerie doesn't know nothing. My bladder fell out.

SCOOPER: This magic doctor says "What does this mean, her bladder fell out." I said "That's what she says, her bladder fell out."

HENNY: My bladder fell out.

SCOOPER: It burns when she pees.

HENNY: It burns when I pee.

SCOOPER *hands her the bottle:* He has an Italian accent so when he comes don't go running out because he's a foreigner. He's a real Latin Lover type is what he sounds like. Take the bottle! And don't go falling in love with him when you hear his Latin accent.

HENNY, *feeling the bottle:* You'd have to be a contortionist in a circus to fit on this. What's wrong with you?

SCOOPER: What's wrong with *me* who finds a doctor who makes house calls? You got a juice bottle?

HENNY: My bladder fell out. I can feel it. Give me your hand. Touch it. Oh God. You can feel it.

SCOOPER: I'm not the doctor. Don't go using me as the doctor.

I'm not going to touch you there. *He goes out of the room.*

HENNY: This doctor's going to lock me up when he sees me. When he sees this bladder.

SCOOPER, *offstage:* The doctor's not the enemy.

HENNY: How do you know? You never saw him before.

SCOOPER: Valerie found him.

HENNY: He's going to run out of here screaming when he sees me.

SCOOPER *comes back into the room:* Doctors don't run out on patients. Crazy patients do the running out so the doctors can't treat them, fix them. Fill this jar. *He puts down a quart-sized juice jar.*

HENNY: It's . . . it's not just my bladder.

SCOOPER *picks up a carton:* Why does an eighty-three-year-old woman have a giant box of Super Kotex? You're not having reverse change of life? Medical marvels. What is this Kotex doing here?

HENNY: I thought it would go away.

SCOOPER: What would go away?

HENNY: I prayed to Saint Jude and said Saint Jude Patron Saint of Lost Causes, Patron Saint of the Impossible, Patron Saint of the Damned, take this away from me.

SCOOPER: Take what away from you?

HENNY: It bleeds and bleeds and I put Kotex over it and stand in front of the window all night in the dark looking up waving a statue of Saint Jude over it so it'll dry by the morning. But it never dries. It never stops bleeding. I sent out for more Kotex. It never stops bleeding. You're hurting my arm!

SCOOPER: What never stops bleeding?

HENNY: I never would've told you about the other incident, except my insides are falling out and I can't pee and I told

you and I could cut my tongue out because it don't hurt
that much when I pee. I could live with it. It's not so bad.

SCOOPER: This other incident?

HENNY: It doesn't hurt. If I could see, I could see it was nothing. But I can't see so I make it up in my mind that it's
more than it is, you see.

SCOOPER: Where is this incident?

HENNY: It's not hide-and-seek, for Christ's sake. I haven't got it
hidden in the back of the stove. It's here. It's me. The incident is me.

SCOOPER: How long?

HENNY: Not long.

SCOOPER: Deal straight. How long?

HENNY: It started in a way I could notice the day you and
Valerie and Ted came out here.

SCOOPER: That was two years ago.

HENNY: It started that day.

SCOOPER: What started that day?

HENNY: The skin broke that day.

SCOOPER: Skin where?

HENNY: It's not important.

SCOOPER: What skin broke?

HENNY: I can deal with this. My Kotex and Saint Jude and I
are very happy. I don't have to pee. If I can just work it
so I don't have to pee, I'm all right.

Door chimes sound.

SCOOPER: He's here. The doctor is here.

HENNY: Send him away.

SCOOPER: We'll hold you down and strip you and find this incident.

HENNY: It feels better. Go away.

SCOOPER: What skin broke?

HENNY, *impatiently:* Oh God. Here. *She opens her blouse. He steps back.* It doesn't look so bad. Does it? Real false alarm. Girl who cried wolf. One day something will be wrong with me and you won't bother to help me because I dragged you out here once before for a little nothing. You're too young to have problems. I don't want to burden you with my problems. You want to send out to that new Italian deli for shrimp salad? They use real shrimp. None of those little plastic pinkies. I buy it to last two days and it's gone before I'm even ready for dinner.

SCOOPER: Oh dear God. Oh Christ. Jesus H fucking Christ.

HENNY: There is no reason for such language. Saint Jude does not like it. Want me to go to the door and tell the doctor to go away? False alarm time? I'll give him five dollars. See my system? The five-dollar bills have one safety pin in them. The tens I have the girl put two safety pins in. The ones are on their own. *The door chime sounds.* Tell him April Fool. Say Saint Jude helped a supposed lost cause make a miraculous recovery.

SCOOPER *goes off. She stands smiling, her blouse open in the light.*

SCOOPER: Doctor, you'd better get in here.

HENNY: No!

BLACKOUT

ACT ONE

———

Deirdre's apartment in the East Sixties. Lots of books. Two couches. Light streams in. A section of the room is used as an office, with Jiffy mailing envelopes, wrapping paper, twine, a stamp machine, and a scale.

DEIRDRE *is in her thirties. Very beautiful. Very intense. She holds a drink and leans forward listening to* SCOOPER. *He sits on the other couch. A packed suitcase is by the door. It is Scooper's.*

SCOOPER: Imagine a peach that had an enormous bite taken out of it.

DEIRDRE: Oh Christ.

SCOOPER: I'm not finished. Then. Then.

DEIRDRE: Calm.

SCOOPER: Was left in the back of a disconnected refrigerator for the winter months and you come back in the spring and open the ice-box door and find the peach rotted where the bite was taken out. This poison gauze. This penicillin rot-mold. You could put your fist into the hole in her breast. The cancer was that deep.

DEIRDRE: Wait.

SCOOPER: She stood there, her blouse off. It's not so bad, she keeps saying. It is not so bad.

DEIRDRE: It's impossible. What you're describing.

SCOOPER: I saw it.

DEIRDRE: Cancer works slowly.

SCOOPER: I am telling you—I can't believe you are not believing me. I pour this out and your response is . . .

DEIRDRE: I'm not saying you're hallucinating. I'm saying cancer works inside, silently. Not like some horror show in a Drive-In.

SCOOPER: She had so neglected herself that the disease was sick of not being noticed. The disease finally burst through her skin. The ulceration was like this screaming flesh, this breast—screaming how loud do you have to go to get noticed?

DEIRDRE: Oh Christ.

SCOOPER: The good part about being that old the metabolism moves so slowly that the cancer takes just that much longer.

DEIRDRE: And she had no medical aid?

SCOOPER: Sure. For two years, she's been laying Kotex over the wound, waving this tan plastic statue of Saint Jude, Patron of Lost Causes, over this small, expanding cavity in her chest, standing all night in the dark privacy of her open window so the midnight air would dry it out.

DEIRDRE: You never noticed?

SCOOPER: I never saw her.

DEIRDRE: In two years?

SCOOPER: She only likes talking on the phone. I can't see her. She can't see me. Gives her equal footing.

DEIRDRE: But her bladder—

SCOOPER: It was her uterus.

DEIRDRE: Oh dear God.

SCOOPER: It fell out.

DEIRDRE: Oh no.

SCOOPER: Eighty-three-year-old muscles give out.

DEIRDRE: But still—

SCOOPER: The doctor who made the house call said this woman is finished. This woman will not make it through the day. It's not so bad. Girl who cried wolf. False alarm." I paid off the doctor. Got Doctor James on the phone. Got her up to Columbia-Presbyterian.

DEIRDRE: The best.

SCOOPER: Doctor James waiting right there. He had a bed waiting, the best surgeon all lined up to see her.

DEIRDRE: That was yesterday?

SCOOPER: That was yesterday.

DEIRDRE: And today she's on the table?

SCOOPER: Right now.

DEIRDRE: It makes *me* feel so well taken care of, like a great fringe benefit, if anything happened to me.

SCOOPER: Thanks to Doctor James.

DEIRDRE: A toast to you.

SCOOPER: To me?

DEIRDRE: To him.

She pours wine. White, chilled. Cool. They toast.

SCOOPER: After two years of lying and hiding.

DEIRDRE: You?

SCOOPER: Her. *They sip.*

DEIRDRE: Poor tragic lady. Outliving her friends. Standing all night at a window. Not trusting any human being enough to reach out.

SCOOPER: Don't forget the statue she's waving over her breast. Significant detail. Saint Jude. Patron of Lost Causes.

DEIRDRE: I suddenly have this image of being blind. Oh God. Never to be able to browse. I could never learn Braille. The skin on my fingers might be too tough to let the words come through.

SCOOPER: She elected to go blind.

DEIRDRE: You don't cast votes to be blind.

SCOOPER: Twenty years ago she did. She marched right up to the polling booth with her glaucoma and cataracts. Her hysteria rendered her untreatable. She looked at my father and me with these eyes turning to milk, the sight curdling out of them. "You're lying to me, it's something worse. Tell me the truth. No, don't tell me the truth. Lie to me." She begged us to lie to her. We said we *were* telling the truth. She said that's the biggest lie. And she invented some exotic disease for herself. And she proceeded to go bonkers and embark on a series of suicide attempts as if the "Guinness Book of Records" suddenly had an opening.

DEIRDRE: And she's still nuts?

SCOOPER: As soon as she went blind, her mind snapped back like the price of gold. She was still alive. Nothing worse had gone wrong with her. She believed the disaster. She was only blind. That she could live with. You become saner much quicker than you go mad. So we had ten years of suicide attempts. And now the last ten she's been feeling her way around like a lost company of *The Miracle Worker*.

DEIRDRE: Your father?

SCOOPER: He stroked out along the way. One day he just short-circuited while she was eating a light bulb . . . or a knife. Stop looking at me that way.

DEIRDRE: Do you find it so difficult taking care of another human being?

SCOOPER: She did it herself.

DEIRDRE: I see why you go to Doctor James.

SCOOPER: Sight is a collaborative act, requiring subject and object working together in trust and tranquillity. You have to tell the doctor what you're seeing and if you're screaming and have flames shooting out of your ears— *He downs his drink. He looks around at all her books.* Are you in publishing?

DEIRDRE: I buy and sell. From estates. First editions.

SCOOPER: You could have two lions in front of your door.

DEIRDRE: How old is she?

SCOOPER: Eighty-three.

DEIRDRE: Then why don't you let her die?

SCOOPER: Because I don't want that solution in me. She is not allowed to take that *out*. Hysteria is not an *out*. Fantasy and panic are not *outs*. I don't want the solution of suicide in my genes. I want courage in my genes. I want strength in my genes. I want seeing problems *through* in my genes. That old lady is going to stay alive and die of old age and plain old-fashioned wearing out. She is not going to be killed by an overactivity of the most valuable thing we have, our imagination. Look, you've got your own problems.

DEIRDRE: No! No! Really! I'm an ear. I love to be an ear.

SCOOPER: Still. He died right here? *He touches her hand.* It must have been a shock.

DEIRDRE: The air conditioner was off. I thought I'd suffocate and I couldn't open any windows, all sealed shut to keep the air conditioning *in*, and I turned on the lights and they flickered and went out and my transistor said it was three A.M. and a hundred degrees. I had this flashlight

and picked up anything to read, just for the reading, just
till it got light . . . "Tess of the D'Urbervilles."

SCOOPER: Thomas Hardy!

DEIRDRE: And Raymond leaps up. His paws cover the text. I
say "Down, Raymond!" And Raymond gasped with the
lack of air and falls over. Right here. Tongue hanging out.
I didn't know what to do. Please let it be light! Finally it
got to be time and I put on this dress and ran out.

SCOOPER: And you come back and he's gone?

DEIRDRE: Wait. The air conditioner's on.

SCOOPER: Who'd break in and kidnap a dead dog?

DEIRDRE: I see! My husband! Of course.

SCOOPER: Your husband?

DEIRDRE: Came back. Saw what happened. Took Raymond up
to the animal hospital for disposal. Or the ASPCA. I'm
glad that's solved. And the air conditioner turned on. Oh
dear, the idea of a thief who breaks in and takes only
dead pets. That's even too strange for a city of strange
tales. Raymond will be back soon and all questions will
be solved.

SCOOPER: Raymond? Will be back?

DEIRDRE: My husband. *She resumes packing books in boxes.* I
really have to get back to work. Charles Dickens off to
Honolulu. *She packs books busily.*

SCOOPER: Your husband and your dog have the same name?

DEIRDRE: That should tell you all you need to know about my
marriage.

SCOOPER: I'm sorry.

DEIRDRE: It's all over. Nothing. Really. Hand me John Updike.

SCOOPER, *bringing her the books:* He must be a great help.

DEIRDRE: John Updike?

SCOOPER: Doctor James.

DEIRDRE: I read somewhere once the reason people have to go

to doctors is the impossibility of the human being to say goodbye.

SCOOPER *picks up some books:* Beautiful bindings. Uncut.

DEIRDRE: I specialize in uncut.

SCOOPER: The weight. The smell. The feel. *She takes the books away from him.*

DEIRDRE: I was touched when you introduced yourself.

SCOOPER: You didn't say "Who is this asshole coming up to me in a Fifth Avenue bookstore?"

DEIRDRE: You're hardly a stranger.

SCOOPER: I stumbled out in the street this morning. Have a wonderful vacation, Doctor James. Don't dare ask him where he's going. Ooops, didn't mean to ask. Should I kiss him? Filial peck on the cheek? Yearly affection. Will he think it's a pass? Decide against. Out in the street. Jesus. Only Nine Fucking Forty Fucking Five A.M. How am I going to get through this day?

DEIRDRE: Already eighty-eight degrees.

SCOOPER: I run to Doubleday's. Fifty-Seventh and Fifth. Wait for it to open. Cool. See what new books have come in since yesterday.

DEIRDRE: But it was like two degrees Celsius.

SCOOPER: Spy. Sex. Show Biz. Something to turn the page.

DEIRDRE: I cannot figure out Celsius.

SCOOPER: And what do I see when I get to the corner? You. Looking in the bookstore window. Waiting for it to open. Your dress swaying slightly. How did your legs find the only breeze?

DEIRDRE: I mean, who *is* Celsius?

SCOOPER: You looked so healthy.

DEIRDRE: I *am* healthy.

SCOOPER: I didn't think you'd.

DEIRDRE: Of course I.

SCOOPER: But you moved away.

DEIRDRE: I didn't think you'd. After months of silence.

SCOOPER: I'd never seen you move. Only sit. The waiting room. Turning pages. Reading copies of *Vogue*.

DEIRDRE: Long gone out of vogue.

SCOOPER: I looked at you staring in the bookshop window and I said this woman and I share the deepest experience of a lifetime and we have never spoken a word. I have even come from a couch that was still warm from you.

DEIRDRE: You followed me.

SCOOPER: To Rizzoli's.

DEIRDRE: The foreign bookstore.

SCOOPER: Is that woman as paralyzed as I am about Doctor James going away for a month?

DEIRDRE: Thumbing through glossy foreign magazines, looking around to see if you were following me. I pick up *Oggi, Paris Match, L'Express.*

SCOOPER: I thought you'd be glad to hear an American voice.

DEIRDRE: Just because someone speaks the same language doesn't mean you can trust them.

SCOOPER: You recognized me.

DEIRDRE: I recognized you.

SCOOPER: "Would you like to have a drink?"

DEIRDRE: "My dog's died and it's eighty-eight degrees and it's just ten A.M. and I don't know what to do."

SCOOPER: "I could help you."

DEIRDRE: "I live around the corner."

SCOOPER: "Around the corner." My God, across the street from Doctor James. I didn't think real people lived on this street. All the Mercedes lined up to haul our pains away. I thought you had to be a shrink to live here.

DEIRDRE: A friend of mine calls this street the Mental Block.

SCOOPER: A close friend?

DEIRDRE, *avoiding the question:* Actually I read it.

SCOOPER: Who's with him now?

DEIRDRE: The mother who drinks.

SCOOPER: Oh Jesus. She once came out of the office and asked me for drink money right in the waiting room.

DEIRDRE: She did the same to me!

SCOOPER: I felt so guilty refusing her.

DEIRDRE: I had to have my session switched.

SCOOPER: Look! There she is!

DEIRDRE: Stand back!

SCOOPER: She's walking so straight.

DEIRDRE, *watching her go:* Sober.

SCOOPER: Healed.

DEIRDRE: A cab pulls up. Out gets the pianist. He runs in, late for his appointment.

SCOOPER: He didn't play for years. That poor genius. Too crazy to play.

DEIRDRE: I have his new record.

SCOOPER: I went to his concert.

DEIRDRE: I was there!

SCOOPER: I thought: Doctor James healed this man so he can play again.

DEIRDRE *puts on a recording. Brilliant Chopin fills the room.*

DEIRDRE: I felt the same thing.

SCOOPER: It's like we're all related.

DEIRDRE: Brothers and sisters sent in for a private loving audience with our father.

SCOOPER, *calling:* We love you, Doctor James!!!!

DEIRDRE: This is no spy turret!

She turns off the music abruptly. SCOOPER *comes away from the window and pours another drink.*

SCOOPER: You must know so much about him.

DEIRDRE: I know he's got a wife.

SCOOPER: Oh, I knew that.

DEIRDRE: Poor Doctor James.

SCOOPER: Poor?

DEIRDRE: That tragic marriage.

SCOOPER: Did he tell you he had a tragic marriage?

DEIRDRE: How could he understand my pain if he didn't have his own? I hear it. There in his voice. That tormented way his fingers rub that birthmark on his hand. Talk about Rorschach tests. I never thought I had any imagination at all until I saw Doctor James's wine-colored birthmark . . . like a magic token transforming me into whatever I want to be. Clouds. Scudding by in the birthmark.

SCOOPER: What birthmark?

DEIRDRE: On his hand.

SCOOPER: Which hand?

DEIRDRE: I lie like this. Look over like this. Yes, the left hand.

SCOOPER: I never noticed any birthmark.

DEIRDRE: Did you notice FDR was in a wheelchair?

SCOOPER: Are you calling Doctor James a cripple?

DEIRDRE: It's the most obvious thing about him.

SCOOPER: You see a spot from luncheon. And you romanticize the coagulation into a birthmark.

DEIRDRE: I have seen that birthmark every day for the past— *number* of years and it is impossible to spill that much gravy in the selfsame spot for the past—*number* of years. Let's not make this one of those events like the song in

Gigi—"I Remember It Well"—based on Colette, where we talk about the same thing and have completely different perceptions of it. You have your Doctor James.

SCOOPER: I have *my* Doctor James.

DEIRDRE: I have my birthmarks. You keep of him whatever you want.

SCOOPER: All I ever see of Doctor James are his wing-tip shoes. I love the guy, but I hate his wing-tip shoes. They're like shoes that belong to some CIA agent.

DEIRDRE: How can you see his wing-tips?

SCOOPER: He crosses his legs. I quick turn up off the couch and look down and see the tips of his shoes.

DEIRDRE: Hating the wings at the tips of his shoes. So fascinating. Hating the fact that Doctor James can fly.

SCOOPER: Do you hear us romanticizing our doctor? We will have to tell him next September. He will laugh.

DEIRDRE: You think?

SCOOPER: You have to take risks.

DEIRDRE: I can never forgive them for taking the month of August off.

SCOOPER: They only do it so we won't run off to other doctors while they're away.

DEIRDRE: As if we'd go to anyone else.

SCOOPER: Sometimes I'll look at a friend in trouble and say Boy, if I trusted you more. Boy, do I have a doctor for you. Boy, could he tie those loose ends up in a minute.

DEIRDRE: But you don't.

SCOOPER: He's my secret weapon.

DEIRDRE: That's not being selfish.

SCOOPER: That's being protective.

DEIRDRE: I think you'd better go.

SCOOPER: Have I said—

DEIRDRE: It might not be healthy talking about our doctor this
way.

SCOOPER: I think he'd be thrilled. I can't wait to tell him.

DEIRDRE: You wouldn't dare tell him!

SCOOPER: To bring Doctor James a new character in my life
that he knows so well? You have to tell him about me.
You'll bring him me. I'll bring him you. To play his version of you against my version of you. To play your me
against his me. It'll be like "The Alexandria Quartet." The
air carbonated with all these realities and people! Poor
Lawrence Durrell. He's become so neglected.

DEIRDRE: Am I a major character or a minor character?

SCOOPER: Friends are always major characters.

DEIRDRE: Friendships are major responsibilities.

SCOOPER: I'm a wonderful friend.

DEIRDRE: Are you a five A.M. friend?

SCOOPER: A five A.M. friend?

DEIRDRE: A friend you can call and say stay on the phone till it
gets light.

SCOOPER: I read a book.

DEIRDRE: Sometimes a book doesn't help.

SCOOPER: You need a voice. I am a five A.M. friend.

They look at each other.

DEIRDRE: Thank you for telling me about your mother, your
father.

SCOOPER: *Life with Father.* Clarence Day.

DEIRDRE: I have that. I love books about families. They read to
me like science fiction.

SCOOPER: You don't have any family?

DEIRDRE: They were killed when I was very young.

SCOOPER: Oh dear.

DEIRDRE: Car crash home from skiing.

SCOOPER: Stowe?

DEIRDRE: Lake Placid.

SCOOPER: Never been to Lake Placid.

DEIRDRE: I went there once.

SCOOPER: I go to Stowe.

DEIRDRE: I have this golden photo of my parents. *She picks up a picture in a frame.* You can see the wit in their eyes. I've learned more about life staring at this picture taken shortly before their deaths trying to riddle out their smiles. Trying to find some injunction in their wrinkled noses. At one point in my life the picture seemed spiritual. I was going to school at a convent. I became a nun for a while.

SCOOPER: You were a nun?

DEIRDRE: I mistook gratitude for a vocation.

SCOOPER: I can't imagine you as a nun.

DEIRDRE: Believe me.

SCOOPER: I'd love to see that picture.

DEIRDRE: I show it to no one. *She puts it away in a drawer.* Doctor James says I read so much to make up their voices reading to me. I hear what I imagine their voices to be telling me about their lives. I read only the finest works. Their voices are very golden in my ear.

SCOOPER: You must be some patient for Doctor James.

DEIRDRE: When you said you'd come from the couch warm with me, you were saying you're in analysis. You don't sit up. I mean, you're not in therapy.

SCOOPER: I'm in analysis.

DEIRDRE: I couldn't talk to you if you were just in therapy.

SCOOPER: You can talk to me.

DEIRDRE: It's so snobbish but I wouldn't have respect for you if you were in therapy— I wish you'd get away from the window. I don't want him looking up and—

SCOOPER: Remember that fat girl—did you ever get a look at her? She must've weighed in at a good four hundred pounds. I used to follow her at one time and I thought the couch would cave in—

DEIRDRE: "Ivanhoe" is an amazing book. It speaks with such an urgent clarity to today. Who'd think Sir Walter Scott would achieve—

SCOOPER: Oh my God, that wasn't you ... was it?

DEIRDRE: Good God, I don't even know who you're talking about. Is that your idea of why people go to Doctor James? He's hardly a fat farm.

SCOOPER: It's just this girl—

DEIRDRE: Why did you go to Doctor James? Weight?

SCOOPER: One little problem that needed tying up.

DEIRDRE: One little problem? No such animal.

SCOOPER: I don't want to tell you anything that'll change your impression of me—

DEIRDRE: Luckily I have no impression of you at all. *She uncorks a wine bottle.*

SCOOPER: I think you're right. *He starts to go.*

DEIRDRE: You were saying why you went—

SCOOPER: He might be angry if he knew we were—

DEIRDRE: Try lying down on the couch—

SCOOPER: I don't want to tell you—

DEIRDRE: It might make it easier.

SCOOPER: He's not lucky enough to get orphans and nuns and husbands and dogs with the same name from me.

DEIRDRE: You're afraid you're not complicated enough? How silly! It's not a competition. How often do we get to share this magic part of our lives?

SCOOPER: It is almost religious with him.

DEIRDRE: Pater Noster. You and I. Brothers. Sisters.

SCOOPER: I'm an only child.

DEIRDRE: Family. That's what we are. We share family secrets.

SCOOPER: I started going to Doctor James because—ahhh. Sherlock Holmes. Beautiful edition . . . *She takes the book from him.* I started going to him because I was so happy.

DEIRDRE: So happy?

SCOOPER: I could live with my mother's suicide attempts and father's strokes. That was like wartime. That was easy. But for one period I stumbled inadvertently into some kind of happiness. Everything was strangely productive and rewarding and simple. I beamed out in this seraphic five A.M. joy why is everything so wonderful? And the Lispenards—*my* five A.M. friends—got me Doctor James's number to find out in a few quick sessions how this wanderer had stumbled into Shangri-La and how he could stay there.

DEIRDRE: And that was—

SCOOPER: Six years ago.

DEIRDRE: Are you still happy?

SCOOPER: Well, one thing led to another. And also Val.

DEIRDRE: Valium?

SCOOPER: Valerie.

DEIRDRE: Valerie?

SCOOPER: My old lady.

DEIRDRE: You don't mean your mother.

SCOOPER: My lady. My girl. My mistress. My blood. My brain. My heart. My wonder.

DEIRDRE: How nice of her to stand by you today.

SCOOPER: No, she's up in New Hampshire putting her kids in camp. Three of them. God, I'll be a father.

DEIRDRE: They're not by you.

SCOOPER: That's a whole other saga. She had Bradley and Kim

and Sophie by Caesarean so she is still tight like a young girl and you come into her so firm and then suddenly it's like coming into St. Peter's in Rome, the way you round a small corner and the entire basilica is wide open in front of you. We have a good time in bed. She'll moan. I'll say "Darling, is that passion?" She says "No, for Christ's sake, I got this Joseph Conrad stuck in my ribs." We both have to have books in our pockets at all times. In our beds. On our walls. *He takes a paperback from his right jacket pocket.* Right now I'm traveling with Rilke. "Duino Elegies." Best poems written this century. *He takes a paperback from the left jacket pocket.* P. G. Wodehouse. "Luck of the Bodkins."

DEIRDRE: Hardly neglected.

SCOOPER: All the time I have to have a book. Words on the eyeball . . . it must create an erotic pressure. The physical rubbing of the words against the eyeball, kneading, prodding, massaging, grazing like this sensuous cow on the green pastures of your eye. And the thought, the illumination, the comprehension! Yes, that's the orgasm. You'd love her.

DEIRDRE: I must meet her.

SCOOPER: I even think of Doctor James as a literary experience. Before Doctor James, my life was pages spilled all over the floor. Grim. Violent. Aimless. He's edited my life into a novel I am so proud to be a part of. Jane Austen. That kind of clarity and effervescence. And intelligence.

DEIRDRE: Nothing's worth it if it's not a great artistic event.

SCOOPER: She wouldn't continue with me unless I kept up the therapy. I started doing the therapy as a bouquet for her. Then the therapy turned into analysis and here we are.

DEIRDRE: She sounds very positive.

SCOOPER: She is so healthy. She's been going to the shrink since she was about two. She has grown up on the couch. Then our affair sent her back into therapy.

DEIRDRE: Not Doctor James.

SCOOPER: No! She goes to group.

DEIRDRE: Group. Eccch.

SCOOPER: And her husband is in another.

DEIRDRE: She's married.

SCOOPER: The Loch Ness Monster lives.

DEIRDRE: Oh dear. Of course. The three children. St. Peter's Basilica.

SCOOPER: She was so unhappy over our affair and guilty that her husband began to feel guilty because he didn't know about our affair and started blaming himself for her grief, so he went into therapy and he was in one group and asked her join him in his group but she was already in another group and she wanted me to join the group her husband was in and then she'd join too, and I said I did not think that was a good idea.

DEIRDRE: I'm with you all the way there.

SCOOPER: I said I'll go to Doctor James for you, but no group analysis.

DEIRDRE: Only teaches you another kind of social chitchat.

SCOOPER: Unless it helps.

DEIRDRE: Of course. And what do your five A.M. friends say to all this?

SCOOPER: The Lispenards? It *is* the Lispenards. Valerie is one half of the Lispenards.

DEIRDRE: And the other half is—

SCOOPER: Ted. My college friend. My business partner. I suddenly see something so clearly. I get in a panic and I can't think straight. You have cleared my head. My God. I see. That vicious rotten human being. Literally rotten.

DEIRDRE: Valerie?

SCOOPER: My mother. She did it on purpose. She knew I was leaving. That's why she waited till yesterday. This operation. This cancer caper. All designed to keep me from going. I don't know how she knew but she knew. Mystic connection.

DEIRDRE: Don't assign her magic powers.

SCOOPER: You don't think she died.

DEIRDRE: On the table?

SCOOPER: Eighty-three. Wouldn't be unheard of. Oh Christ.

DEIRDRE: Believe it or not, mastectomy is simple surgery.

SCOOPER: May I use your phone? *He begins dialing.*

DEIRDRE: The breast doesn't involve any major body function like breathing or digesting.

SCOOPER *speaks into the phone:* I'm trying to get information on the outcome of an operation? Could you connect me with— *To Deirdre:* They put me on hold.

DEIRDRE: She'll be all right.

SCOOPER: That breast nursed me. Fed me. My first connection. All the time I spend pursuing wombs, hidden under infinities of skirts, entry to that warm darkness, and to see what I'm searching for, hanging there. Light shining on what no light should ever shine. This fucking old lady thinks it's her bladder. If I'm conceived out of a bladder, what does that make me? Get me off hold! Operator! Operator! *He snaps the wine glass in his hand.* Godammit!!!

DEIRDRE *runs out of the room.*

SCOOPER: I want the recovery room! Okay. Back on hold. If that's the way you want it.

DEIRDRE *returns with a basin of water and bandages. She takes his hand and washes the cut.*

DEIRDRE: "All happy families are alike:" I don't know about you but I find Tolstoi very comforting.

SCOOPER: Are you a nurse?

DEIRDRE, *avoiding the question:* I hope you're not a concert pianist. Don't have to give a concert tonight.

SCOOPER: I'm an analyst.

DEIRDRE: But Doctor James—

SCOOPER: A computer analyst. Don't laugh.

DEIRDRE: I just had this mental image of all these angst-ridden computers jumping up on your couch. Help me! Help me!

SCOOPER: This customer calls me up, falling apart like the fifth floor at Bellevue. And he tells me his secretary wiped out his file. "Calm down," I say. "She probably only switched directories on you. Re-boot the disc. Do a hardware re-boot. Do Control Alternate Delete. Then the AutoExec will reset the default and everything will be there when the spread sheet looks for it." And that's how I speak all day.

DEIRDRE: What does Hanna Arendt say? "Without passport and language we are nothing."

SCOOPER: Well, exactly. I love the way the light streams in your apartment.

DEIRDRE: I said once before I died I'd finally live in a place filled with light.

SCOOPER: Heat banging its fists against the window trying to get in. *Into the phone.* Operator! I'm here! Don't go away! *But she has.* Should I dial again?

DEIRDRE: Hang on there.

SCOOPER: O.K. Oh God. *He buries his face in his hands. Pause.*

DEIRDRE: You know who's tragically neglected? The Japanese. Kawabata.

SCOOPER: Is he the one with the private army who disemboweled himself?

DEIRDRE: That's Mishima.

SCOOPER: Is Kawabata the one who has the Japanese married couple traveling to all the puppet shows in Japan? A dying art to mirror a dying marriage?

DEIRDRE: No, that's Tanazaki.

SCOOPER: Is Kawabata the one who writes about the whorehouse where an old man rents drugged young girls and holds them in his arms all night, never fucking them. Just holding them.

DEIRDRE: That's Kawabata.

SCOOPER: So *that's* Kawabata. So neglected.

DEIRDRE: He won the Nobel Prize.

SCOOPER, *disdainful:* Pearl Buck won the Nobel Prize. What did you think about Isaac Bashevis Singer winning the Nobel Prize?

DEIRDRE: I cut something out of *TV Guide*. "Dick Cavett Show. Dick's guest tonight will be the singer, Isaac Bashevis."

SCOOPER: You have to show that to me.

DEIRDRE: I showed it to Saul Bellow and he was sending it out for Christmas cards.

SCOOPER: You know Saul Bellow?????

DEIRDRE: Well . . .

SCOOPER: You know someone who won the Nobel Prize?????

DEIRDRE: Oh, he's not my only Nobel Prize winner. I cradled Samuel Beckett in my arms right over there. Norman Mailer passed out there. I have authors in and out of here.

SCOOPER, *into the phone:* Yes? I'm calling to see if my mother has come down from surgery yet? I know you're busy but —her name is—has she even gone into surgery? I'm not trying to sell this info to the Chinese, believe me. You

advise me not to stay at the hospital while the operation's
on but then you won't—she's blind, she'll wake up and
not know where—there was a brownout?

DEIRDRE: Happened here this morning. Lights just dim.

SCOOPER: Nobody's gone into surgery yet? When are they
going into surgery? I have a plane to catch! *He slams the
phone down.* She hasn't even gone in yet.

DEIRDRE: Leaving?

SCOOPER: Five o'clock.

DEIRDRE: Tonight?

SCOOPER: Haiti.

DEIRDRE: This time of year?

SCOOPER: She's trying to stop me.

DEIRDRE: The sidewalks are buckling and you're going to the
jungle?

SCOOPER: It's so blindingly clear.

DEIRDRE: Don't people usually go to Haiti in the winter?

SCOOPER: She's been saving that breast to whip out just at an
instant like this.

DEIRDRE: The heat in August. Frying pan. Fire.

SCOOPER: Hiding that whammy there in her bra.

DEIRDRE: But I suppose it's a different kind of heat.

SCOOPER: To stop me with guilt. Stop me with caring.

DEIRDRE: But people *always* say a different kind of heat.

SCOOPER: The caring is over.

DEIRDRE: Still hot is hot.

SCOOPER: My heart is sealed up.

DEIRDRE: On the other hand—

SCOOPER: I have to keep reminding myself she is a crazy old
lady crippled by fear. Two years at a window waving
plastic statues of fictional saints over a bleeding breast.
God, Haiti. Tropic. Lush. She's not stopping me. Olaff-
son's Hotel. Great white Victorian bric-a-brac ginger-

bread hotel there in the jungle. Victorian. Voodoo. Volcanoes.

DEIRDRE: If you need any Valium.

SCOOPER: I'll have Valerie.

DEIRDRE: You're taking Valerie?

SCOOPER: Our first trip together. Finally. The decision.

DEIRDRE: What does her husband say to all this?

SCOOPER: We haven't told him yet. We've left a letter for him at his group tonight. We felt that was the kindest thing to do. He goes right from work to group. He couldn't read a letter like the one we've left him alone. He's so dependent on his group. Poor weak . . . don't get me started on Ted.

DEIRDRE: Should be an interesting session.

SCOOPER: In a way I'd like to be there. What was Hemingway's phrase? Grace under pressure? I don't think Ted Lispenard will personify grace under pressure.

DEIRDRE: And you'll be in Haiti.

SCOOPER: Four weeks.

DEIRDRE: The time Doctor James is away.

SCOOPER: Her sister will take the kids. When we get back we'll start looking for a place in Maine. Get out of this neurotic city. Find a beat-up ramshackle house by the sea. Remodel it. Books. Music. Comfort. Valerie says she wants a house like us. Simple on the outside. But inside. Inside! We have this dream of buying up every book in Maine.

DEIRDRE: That shouldn't be hard.

SCOOPER: Open the world's greatest bookstore. Get out of computers and machinery. Publish newsletters written by people telling what books they love. A bookstore open twenty-four hours a day.

DEIRDRE: Like L. L. Bean.

SCOOPER: Yes! People will flock to us from all over the world and we'll grow and grow until one day the entire town is one bookstore.

DEIRDRE: The elephant graveyard.

SCOOPER: A Vatican of books. "If we don't have it, they didn't write it."

DEIRDRE: You'll finish your treatment?

SCOOPER: Finishing my treatment is not the most important thing in the world. I'm almost finished with Doctor James anyway. Except for this one dream I have that even the great dream-decipherer himself can't figure out.

DEIRDRE: Please? I might be able to help—

SCOOPER: I am this little boy. All dressed up.

DEIRDRE: New clothes. Masquerade.

SCOOPER: A strange city.

DEIRDRE: Outsider. Go on.

SCOOPER: Facing a strange man.

DEIRDRE: And you're a small child. And it's not your father. Hmmm.

SCOOPER: And my mother who is all dolled up—

DEIRDRE: A new beginning?

SCOOPER: Picks me up and begins hitting this man with me.

DEIRDRE: Using you as a weapon?

SCOOPER: And she's screaming You neglected me! You neglected me!

DEIRDRE: And then you wake up?

SCOOPER: It's so alive in my mind.

DEIRDRE: I could figure that out.

SCOOPER: I really wish you wouldn't.

DEIRDRE: Strange city. Outsider. A dream of betrayal.

SCOOPER: I didn't say betrayal. I said neglect.

DEIRDRE: Neglect is always betrayal.

SCOOPER: Is that a quote?

DEIRDRE: That's a belief.

SCOOPER: If he can't figure it out—talk about "Pride and Preju-
    dice"—I don't think you can. Stay out of it. O.K.?

DEIRDRE: I'll butt out of your head. Fine.

SCOOPER: But I know the key to everything is in that dream.

DEIRDRE: Oh, I see! If you solve the dream, you'll have to leave
    him.

SCOOPER: I want to leave him!

DEIRDRE: I didn't say you didn't.

SCOOPER: He's getting a postcard from me with a volcano on it
    and the message reads Doctor, see this volcano? This is
    me . . . Suppose she's dead. Suppose she died?

He picks up the phone and dials: Columbia-Presbyterian—is
this? What number have I? *He puts the phone down in agony,
then gets his face into a big smile. He lifts the phone again.*

Ted. Hi! What are you doing home? No, my fingers
were just dialing. And I dialed. Summer cold? Oh no.
They're the worst. Go back to sleep. You shouldn't answer
the phone if you're sick. Are you going to group tonight?
No, you mustn't miss that. Take care. Oh. Valerie called?
What time did she leave for New Hampshire? Great.
Listen, thank you for the flowers. She was barely in the
hospital when the flowers arrived. Really sweet. I don't
know yet. But the best doctors. Could you do me a favor?
Valerie wanted a report on how my mother is. I'm not at
home. Could you give her the number where I'll be.
680-3779. I'll be here. A friend. I'll call later. *He hangs
up. He is furious.* Asshole. You don't send flowers to a
blind person. You treat her senses. You send candy. That's
Ted in a nutshell. Oh, fuck. This atmosphere of lying.
Everyday for the past five years, living life with this Pav-

lovian smile trapped on my face. Inside I'm dying. A
Madame Tussaud's perfect wax smile.

DEIRDRE *turns away from him. She looks back at him with
disdain.*

DEIRDRE: Betraying your five A.M. friends.
SCOOPER: It didn't seem like betraying. The love sweetened
everything.
DEIRDRE: You mean it poisoned everything. Like the silence of
your mother's sickness.
SCOOPER, *reaching for a book:* Joseph Conrad. "Chance"! This
is one of the books stuck in Valerie's ribs.
DEIRDRE, *disillusioned:* One of the great neglected master-
pieces.
SCOOPER: I love this damned book.
DEIRDRE: So did I.
SCOOPER: "Life demands a man and a woman." *He searches
through the book.*
DEIRDRE: Page 432. "Pairing off is the fate of mankind."
SCOOPER, *reading:* "If two beings thrown together, mutually
attract . . . voluntarily stop short of the—the *embrace*—"
DEIRDRE, *quoting:* "they are committing a sin against life.
The call of which is simple."
BOTH: "Perhaps sacred."

A pause. They look at each other.

SCOOPER: It's taken Valerie and me five years to get to this day.
I don't want to get mixed up with another married lady.
DEIRDRE: I'm not married.
SCOOPER: Raymond.
DEIRDRE: There is no Raymond. I only told you that—a girl
has to be—a woman has to be—I call myself a woman

when I'm working, but when I'm alone in this apartment, I'm a girl. A girl has to be careful. I don't know you. A patient. I don't know what you're seeing him for. You might be a psychopath. I wanted you to think someone was coming home.

SCOOPER: You wear a wedding ring.

DEIRDRE: A friend advised me to. It avoids hassles.

SCOOPER: A close friend?

DEIRDRE: What time is your plane?

SCOOPER: Five o'clock.

DEIRDRE: Busy day. Very active. Very healthy. Haiti. "Comedians."

SCOOPER: I don't know who's playing down there.

DEIRDRE: Graham Greene. Novel. Haiti. In this pile.

SCOOPER: I've never read that.

DEIRDRE: I'd like to give it to you.

SCOOPER: Sign it?

DEIRDRE, *digging angrily in the stacks:* Where the fuck is it? Here. In the Evelyn Waugh pile. That's neglected. When one author ends up in another author's pile.

SCOOPER: They're all English. Easy mistake.

DEIRDRE: Your hand is all right?

SCOOPER: All fine.

DEIRDRE, *writing in the book:* "Be careful in the jungle."

SCOOPER: You sound like my mother.

DEIRDRE: Why did you pick me up today?

SCOOPER: I told you. The breeze around your legs—

DEIRDRE: We shared the same waiting room for so many months in silence. I spend so many sessions asking Doctor James, Why isn't that man looking at me? I even got it into my head that Doctor James had hired you to drive me mad, to ignore me, to come for your session even before my session.

SCOOPER: I came to prepare. To calm myself. A quiet place to read.

DEIRDRE: You'd loom outside that door. I'd be inside on the couch. You'd be out there, doing God knows what. Listening at the door. Laughing at me.

SCOOPER: Never. I was reading.

DEIRDRE: I begged Doctor James to change appointments. Please! I don't want to be annihilated by that man.

SCOOPER: And he only said Why does the presence of that man annoy you?

DEIRDRE: You *were* listening.

SCOOPER: How could I hear with his air conditioner on?

DEIRDRE: You became my father. My lovers. My teachers. My uncles. My bosses. Every man who's ever gone out of his way to ignore me. I found myself dressing for you. Would he notice this? I'll show him. I would stand up naked in this window and wait for you to come out of your appointment. I'd do hypnotism things. Now he'll look up. Now he'll see me.

SCOOPER: I was deep in my own problems.

DEIRDRE: So you missed my breakdown.

SCOOPER: When was it?

DEIRDRE: Last October.

SCOOPER: Last October. That was a rough time for me last October.

DEIRDRE: I had one of the world's greatest uninstitutionalized breakdowns with weeping and moaning and Doctor James pulling magic tricks out of the air to keep me out of a hospital and you sit there turning the pages.

SCOOPER: I was reading Herman Melville.

DEIRDRE: You ignore me for eleven months and today you are suddenly obsessed with unculminated desire to pick me up.

SCOOPER: You're an attractive woman.

DEIRDRE: I have been for the last eleven months. It's still the same flesh.

SCOOPER: Edith Wharton says beauty is genius of the skin.

DEIRDRE: Did Doctor James say "Take her? She's lonely. She's mad. She's out roaming the streets right now. My going-away present from doctor to patient. I can't mess around with her because of the Hippocratic Oath, but you give her a good boff for me." Is that what the mind butcher said to you? Is that how you spend your sessions? Talking about me? How many other patients has old stud Doctor James fixed you up with? The mother who drinks? Is she another one of your old discards? You are wasting your forty bucks an hour. The two of you. Two Freudian mind fuckers. He tells you all my secrets? The two of you having a bloody good laugh on my account? I thought you and I *shared* Doctor James. Brothers and sisters? Going in to visit our father? Brothers and sisters? Hah!

SCOOPER: Forty dollars an hour?

DEIRDRE: I suddenly understand incest.

SCOOPER: Forty dollars an hour? ? ? ?

DEIRDRE: You have successfully ruined Doctor James for this analysand. I can never go back to him again.

SCOOPER: He charges me fifty dollars an hour.

DEIRDRE: Fifty dollars an hour?

SCOOPER: He charges you forty dollars an hour?

DEIRDRE: Forty.

SCOOPER: Why does he charge me fifty?

DEIRDRE: He charges you fifty?

SCOOPER: Fifty and forty? It doesn't seem fair.

DEIRDRE: He charges me forty because I am his favorite patient.

SCOOPER: Don't say that.

DEIRDRE: Sometimes he doesn't even charge me. Sometimes he says you are so interesting, I should be giving you money just for the privilege of listening to you pour out your heart.

SCOOPER: He doesn't say that.

DEIRDRE: No, he doesn't.

SCOOPER: But he does charge you forty.

DEIRDRE: Forty.

SCOOPER: How many days a week?

DEIRDRE: Five.

SCOOPER: How many years?

DEIRDRE: Eight.

SCOOPER: You must be very sick.

DEIRDRE: How long for you?

SCOOPER: Six.

DEIRDRE: How many days a week?

SCOOPER: The three I see you.

DEIRDRE: Oh, therapy. You're only in therapy.

SCOOPER: I'm in analysis.

DEIRDRE: Three days a week? Gerber's Baby Food analysis. On the other hand, we have me! Five days a week! Depths of my psyche! Sonar waves into my soul! Psychic barium cocktails.

SCOOPER: Wait. You go early in the morning.

DEIRDRE: Gallop straight from my dreams to the couch.

SCOOPER: Oh, I know what you're in.

DEIRDRE: Doctor can't wait to start off his day with a high.

SCOOPER: You're in supportive analysis.

DEIRDRE: Deep classical.

SCOOPER: You're one of those sad neurotics who have to go first thing in the morning just to get enough courage—

DEIRDRE, *holding her ears:* What Beethoven is to the sonata, I am to the couch!

SCOOPER: —just to get through the day.

DEIRDRE: I am *not* in supportive.

SCOOPER: You're one of those cripples who can only take life in twenty-four-hour doses. Then off to daddy.

DEIRDRE: I am very strong.

SCOOPER: When did he say you were strong?

DEIRDRE: You're the one who listens at the door. You tell me.

SCOOPER: He hardly says anything ever to me.

DEIRDRE: To me he gives wonders.

SCOOPER: All I know is I possess enough strength to get through a simple day.

DEIRDRE: To me he tells secrets of living.

SCOOPER: I only need him three days a week.

DEIRDRE: He reads me from the Secret Freud Handbook.

SCOOPER: I don't use him for a crutch.

DEIRDRE: He wants me to be free.

SCOOPER: I don't think Doctor James likes the kind of patient who uses him for a crutch.

DEIRDRE: He says Deirdre, I learn from you!

SCOOPER: He has you first just to get the worst out of the way.

DEIRDRE: It boils down to this.

SCOOPER: He's not helping you if he's charging you charity fees.

DEIRDRE: I am in analysis. You are in therapy. You are going to him for one specific problem. Your girlfriend. Your mother. I am going to him for my whole life. All the fantasies I wasted on you. I had you trapped in this Dostoevskian turmoil. A fellow tormentee. Someone who is my match. Someone who understands. What do I get picked up by? Cuticle despair. Is that why the little baby's going to Doctor James? His little cuticle hurts?

SCOOPER: You're being very hostile.

DEIRDRE: You have discovered the mouth of the River Hostility.
   You are drowning in the Great Lakes of Hostility.

SCOOPER: Don't say that.

DEIRDRE: Oh, little baby can dish it out. But little baby can't
   take it. You want to know why I'm spending the best
   years of my life on Doctor James's couch? And it looks
   like my sunset years. You want to know the magic event
   that will clarify everything for you? Little magic key
   revelations? I hurt someone. Hurt them very badly.

SCOOPER: You don't mean breaking hearts.

DEIRDRE: We both share a relationship of a long nature with
   a married person. *She lights a cigarette.*

SCOOPER: Of which sex?

DEIRDRE: A married person. This married person sat in a hotel
   room and told me this person was going back to their
   mate. Finally. Over. I had trouble hearing because the
   ashtray on the table between us started talking to me.
   The ashtray was empty because both of us had stopped
   smoking. We had met at a SmokEnders clinic and it
   made us think we had a great deal in common and we
   had both not smoked for a long time now and I felt
   proud of that. But now words like Over and Returning
   became our vocabularies' main themes and this ashtray
   says to me Just because you don't smoke anymore doesn't
   mean you have to neglect me. And the ashtray starts
   singing in this lovely clear voice the old Jerome Kern
   standard "Why Was I Born?" And this person whose
   lungs I have helped clear packs a suitcase and calls room
   service and orders a pack of cigarettes. Camels. Lucky
   Strikes. Anything without a filter. And I knew it was
   over. And we sat there a long time. Room service brings
   the smokes. A pot of decaffeinated coffee. And the ashtray
   suddenly stops singing and says I'll tell you why you were

born. To free yourself. Do it. Use me! I picked up the
ashtray and could see the person all distorted in its glass
base. I brought it down on the side of this person's
head.

SCOOPER: Did you kill this person?

DEIRDRE: The person turned to light the cigarette. The match
flew out of my friend's hand and landed on blue pajamas
which I thought were silk but were this incendiary Orlon
and the suitcase burst into flame and I threw the de-caf
coffee on the bed and put out the fire and called room
service to take care of this person with the gash on the
person's head and in a secret way found Doctor James
and have been going to him everyday since that day.

SCOOPER: This person. Was it a man or a woman?

DEIRDRE: It was a man, goddamit. *She picks up an ashtray.*
A man! You're like every other man I ever met in my
life. You come on like this great oral aggressive, but at
heart you're this anal retentive . . .

SCOOPER: I think . . . really wish you would put that down.
I'm not like your friend. I stopped smoking and have not
started up. Put it down. *She puts the ashtray down quietly.*
I saw you in the waiting room. I couldn't look at you
because of the desperation smeared all over your face.
I said Is that what I look like?

DEIRDRE: Then you must have felt some sympathy for me. If
you saw my agony.

SCOOPER: There's no sympathy in a doctor's waiting room.
Only me next. Me next. I picked you up today because
I was sad Doctor James was leaving, crazy because I am
finally leaving with the woman I love after a trillion
years of waiting. I'm losing a close friend, Ted, my old
college roommate. And my mother's body bursts open
and I'm furious at her for not trusting me enough to

tell me two years ago and I see you, beside the books, and I just wanted to connect to you.

DEIRDRE: E. M. Forster says that. Connect. Only connect.

SCOOPER: Fuck E. M. Forster. I just wanted to sit down and share.

DEIRDRE: And what did you find out?

SCOOPER: That I'm being overcharged.

DEIRDRE: I'm sorry I said you were only in therapy.

SCOOPER: It's the meanest thing anybody ever said to me.

DEIRDRE: Well, if that's the meanest thing—

SCOOPER: I'd better go. Up to the hospital. Find out what I can before I'm off. *He picks up his suitcase and stands at the door.* We'll meet again.

DEIRDRE: You'll be all healthy, living with the world's most perfect woman. I don't think we'll meet.

SCOOPER: Thank you for the Greene. *He starts to go.*

DEIRDRE: My father lives in New Jersey.

SCOOPER, *pausing:* Recuperating from his death in the Lake Placid car crash?

DEIRDRE: He lives in a nursing home. Which is why I asked you before if your mother was in a nursing home. If I can help in any way. We both share a guilt about the way we neglected a parent.

SCOOPER: I haven't neglected anybody . . .

DEIRDRE: It's a very good nursing home. It's a lot but the Medicare helps out. My father was in the Mafia. You don't have to be Italian to be in the Mafia. He was in charge of all the pinball machines in the state of New Jersey. Atlantic City. Up through the Jersey shore. I didn't mind that. But when I was twenty, I found out that he had gone over to drugs and was pushing drugs. Fairly large quantities in the same areas where he previously had had the pinballs . . . I found that out inad-

vertently. He kept things from me. Loved that I read
and was smart. But when I found out about the drugs.
Heroin. Did I tell you it was heroin? I blew the whistle
on him. I called the FBI. They arrested him. It was on
the front pages of lots of papers. Daughter Turns in
Father. Do you remember me? Sometimes for a while
after that, people would recognize my face. I wrote a book
about it.

SCOOPER, *in awe:* You wrote one of *these?*

DEIRDRE: Long before the day of the big paperback sale. Still I
got an advance you'd call tidy. "Turn-In: The Story of a
Daughter."

SCOOPER: I don't know it.

DEIRDRE: Talk about neglected. It never took off the way they
hoped. Out of print. No copies.

> The FBI gave me a new identity. After I named names
> and after I named Papa, our family no longer existed. I
> no longer had the right to use my family name.

SCOOPER: Deirdre is not your name?

DEIRDRE: No, that's all I kept. Deirdre I kept. But this hair . . .
this face . . . this body, all new.

SCOOPER: All new?

DEIRDRE: The FBI set me up here. Helped me get started.

SCOOPER: This is a government bookstore?

DEIRDRE: No. Then they left me on my own. All I had was my
books.

SCOOPER: Do you miss your old life? My god, losing everything.
You're quite beautiful now. They did . . . whoever, a wonderful job.

DEIRDRE: Do I miss my old life? No, strangely, what I miss . . .
the moment I can't lose is the moment I turned my father
in. The moment I called.

SCOOPER: You can't do that too often.

DEIRDRE: I know, and now that he's not available, I do the next
best thing.

SCOOPER: Which is?

DEIRDRE: I call up the spouses of authors who mean the world
to me.

SCOOPER: And say what?

DEIRDRE: Look up Norman Mailer. I know how to sow the
seeds.

SCOOPER *looks through the Rolodex.*

SCOOPER: My god, the names here; Saul Bellow. William
Styron.

DEIRDRE: Dial Norman Mailer.

SCOOPER: Brooklyn. 718 area code. SCOOPER *dials the phone.* It's
ringing.

DEIRDRE *takes the phone:* Mrs. Mailer? Mrs. Norman Mailer?
Yes. Could you please give Norman—I mean Mr. Mailer
—a message? Tell him it's Deirdre calling. Tell him
his *book* is ready. Tell him his special order is ready.
The special order. The one he was dying for. *She hangs
up.*

SCOOPER: But you could get him in trouble.

DEIRDRE: Why do you think he's been married so many times?

SCOOPER: You are incredible. Do another one.

DEIRDRE: Spin the Rolodex!

SCOOPER *spins:* Doctorow, E. L.

DEIRDRE: Dial!

SCOOPER *dials:* It's a machine.

DEIRDRE *takes the phone:* Edgar. It's Deirdre waiting for you
again and again and again, Edgar, we can repeat the past.
Yes. Yes. Yes. *She hangs up.*

SCOOPER: I want to try one!

SCOOPER *finds a name and dials.*

SCOOPER: May I speak to Joan Didion? Is this her husband? Yes, Mr. Dunne, I'd like to leave a message. Tell her it's . . . Tell her it's Herman Melville and I want to hear Joan cry out "Omoo" once more. I want to hear her cry out "Typee." Do you have that? "Omoo! Typee!" *He hangs up.* Holy Christ, this is fantastic! I want to call Joyce Carol Oates!

DEIRDRE *takes phone from him:* My father was in the Big House for a long time.

SCOOPER: Is he still in the Big House?

DEIRDRE: He's out now. He developed this very bad arthritis in prison. And his stomach is gone from taking so many aspirins for his arthritis. I'm hoping one day before he dies we can clear the books. He will lean over and take my hand and say I understand why you did what you did. So I go out there every weekend, sit there, read. Out loud. Wait for the scene. That moment that will clarify all. I've gone through James Joyce and Wallace Stevens.

SCOOPER: Does a Mafia Chief understand it?

DEIRDRE: I don't know. I only hope he'll hear the voice underneath. English has the largest vocabulary of any language and perhaps one day I'll come up with the right combination and my father will forgive me for putting him away for ten years in the slammer.

SCOOPER: You put a lot of faith in the language.

DEIRDRE: Yes. Yes, I do. *She throws herself into his arms.*

SCOOPER: What you've been through. I'd like to show you how much I care for you.

DEIRDRE *undoes his tie. Through her tears:* Care for Dr. James. Care for our work.

SCOOPER: What are you reading to your father now?

DEIRDRE *unbuttons his collar button:* The South Americans.

SCOOPER *pulls the tie off his shirt:* Don't get me started on the South Americans.

DEIRDRE: Jorge Amado. *She turns out light.*

SCOOPER *undresses as fast as he can:* "The Two Loves of Doña Flor."

DEIRDRE *opens bed:* "Gabriella Clove and Cinnamon."

SCOOPER *undoes his tie:* "A Hundred Years of Solitude."

DEIRDRE *steps out of the other shoe:* Marquez is hardly neglected.

SCOOPER *takes off a shoe:* A cult book.

DEIRDRE *unbuttons her blouse:* But not neglected. Overpraised.

SCOOPER *unbuttons his shirt:* But perfect.

DEIRDRE *drawing the shades:* Of its kind. *The room is dark.* But like all cult books ultimately overpraised.

SCOOPER: Think of me as an eclipse.

DEIRDRE: An eclipse?

SCOOPER, *undressing her:* Let me move into your orbit. Let me blot out the vision of your father. Oh God—you poor girl—what you've been through—I'd like to show you how much I care for you— *They are on the couch.*

DEIRDRE: Care for Doctor James, care for our work—

SCOOPER: Care for our meeting—

DEIDRE: Have you ever been to South America?

SCOOPER: No. No. But emotionally I identify with the South Americans.

DEIRDRE: I'd like to put another woman's body between you and the image of that half-rotten peach. That poisoned gauze. Restore the womb to its proper dark place. Do you read Valéry?

SCOOPER: Do I read to Valerie?

DEIRDRE: Paul Valéry.

SCOOPER: I don't read French.

DEIRDRE: I don't either.

SCOOPER: Your first edition of Byron.

DEIRDRE: Shall we read it?

SCOOPER: It's uncut. *She takes a paper knife.* It'll reduce the
value. I'll cut just one page. *He takes the paper knife
from her. He takes one of the Byron volumes. He slices
the page, opens the book carefully and reads:* "But some
are dead and some are gone And some are scattered and
alone And some are rebels on the hills . . ." *He gives her
the book and the knife. She slices open a page and reads.*

DEIRDRE: Ahhh. He says, "Had Orpheus fiddled at the present
hour He'd see lions waltzing in the tower."

SCOOPER: The pressure.

DEIRDRE: The sound.

SCOOPER: The pages resist.

DEIRDRE: Gentle. *She cuts another page.*

SCOOPER: Feels good. *He cuts another page.*

DEIRDRE: Firm. *She cuts another page.*

SCOOPER: Slice. *He cuts another page.*

DEIRDRE: The odor.

SCOOPER: The feel.

DEIRDRE: The paper.

SCOOPER: The binding.

DEIRDRE: The print.

SCOOPER: The ink.

DEIRDRE: So neglected.

SCOOPER: So neglected.

*They each cut a page. They drop the books. They embrace
hungrily. Dark. Close shades. Quiet. The phone rings. It rings.*

DEIRDRE: No.

SCOOPER *picks up the phone:* Yes? Valerie! DEIRDRE *turns on the light.* SCOOPER *holds his shirt in front of him.* How was New Hampshire? *He signals Deirdre to turn off that light. Darkness again.* I'm just at a friend's house. The operation—I don't know—there was a brownout. Chicken pox? What are you talking about. She has cancer. Bradley has chicken pox? *He turns on the light. He now has his shorts and one stocking on.* DEIRDRE *lies on the couch, the throw on the couch over her, her arms over her eyes.* They turned you back from the camp? Sophie might have chicken pox? Kim might have it? They're all home with you? You drove all the way up to New Hampshire with them and now they're all back with you? Can't your sister— *He turns the light off. Blackness.* It's very difficult to talk right now. Why didn't you give him shots? You have no right to say that—what are you saying? Our affair took up so much time that you have neglected your kids? Stop crying. *He turns the light back on. He is pacing back and forth. He now has his shirt on.* Chicken pox is not dangerous. You are not a terrible woman. I don't care if you've never had chicken pox. *I've* never had chicken pox. We can still get on the plane. We'll start a world-wide epidemic of chicken pox. I don't care. I want us to be off. Don't cry, Val! Val! Valerie! Hi, Ted. Listen, Ted, we might as well cut the shit—Valerie is not unpacking from New Hampshire. Those bags are for me. She is packing for me. Ted, you might as well know. Valerie and I are going to Haiti tonight. When you get to your group, you'll find a letter from us. Ted, Valerie and I—Val, get off the extension. Let me tell him! Valerie, I'll be right over there to pick you up. Ted, we have been screwing right under your nose for the past five years. Valerie, put that phone down. Valerie, it's the only time we can go. With the doctor. I've met a wonderful person who'll help us with our books. Valerie? I'll be right over. Ted. Put Valerie on. Hello? *He hangs up. Pause.* Her kid's got chicken pox.

DEIRDRE, *so pleased:* Oh. I'm sorry.

SCOOPER: Psychosomatic chicken pox.

DEIRDRE: What a month we can have! New York in August! You can get into any restaurant. Movies are empty and cool! Movies! We'll see every movie in town and get icicles on us from watching—should we see only films adapted from books and sit in the theater with flashlights and read along with the movie? Day trips to the beach! Museums! *She looks out the window.* The pianist comes out. Is he weeping? No, the pianist is dancing! He is healed! *She puts on the Chopin again.* When you said you were reading Rilke, I couldn't believe it. I fell in love with you at that moment. I can mark my love.

SCOOPER: I just picked up Rilke. I'm not familiar with Rilke.

DEIRDRE: Rilke couldn't write for ten years. But he trusted his angels would return to him. And they did. That book in your pocket, "The Duino Elegies." That's the only reason we're going to Doctor James. To keep ourselves open so we can recognize our angels when they finally show up. We have been given a gift!

SCOOPER: She didn't leave him.

DEIRDRE: One day you will write that lady such a thank you note!

SCOOPER: She promised she'd leave him.

DEIRDRE: And people make promises and people break promises—

SCOOPER: You know what I blame it all on?

DEIRDRE: Don't blame it on anybody. To be our ages and unattached.

SCOOPER: I never read a book that had a thing to do with my life. *He stacks books in a pile as tall as he is.*

DEIRDRE: Don't you hear me? *She turns off the music.*

SCOOPER: We're the subsidiary characters in everybody's lives. That's the joke, the joke of our lives. We spend all our time babbling to Herr Doktor across the street about ourselves and we don't figure in anyone's life. I bring my life to Doctor James and we turn my life into a lullaby until I am as fictional to myself as any one of these books are to me. *He punches the pile of books and begins ripping them.* I wish I were blind! And illiterate! I wish I could rip all the sight out of my head. *He rips a pile of books.* Were you a nun? Were you an orphan! Is your father in the Mafia! Are you even in books!

DEIRDRE *throws herself on her books:* Don't rip my books! Stop it!

SCOOPER *pushes her out of the way. She falls. He destroys lots of books.*

DEIRDRE: My ankle!

SCOOPER: I want to get all this fiction out of my eyes!

DEIRDRE *picks up the paper knife. She stabs him. He is in such a fury he doesn't even feel it.*

SCOOPER: Throw them all out the window!

SCOOPER *opens the curtains to heave the books through the glass. His shirt is covered with blood.* DEIRDRE *is hysterical.* SCOOPER *stops.*

SCOOPER: There's Doctor James. Coming out of his office.

DEIRDRE, *hopping to the window:* Who's driving the blue Mercedes?

SCOOPER: A woman.

DEIRDRE: Three children.

SCOOPER: They put the luggage in the trunk.

DEIRDRE: He kisses them all.

SCOOPER: He gets in the driver's seat.

DEIRDRE: They drive away.

SCOOPER: Come back.

DEIRDRE: Come back!

SCOOPER: Doctor James, come back!

DEIRDRE: Doctor James, come back!

They press against the glass.

SCOOPER: I see the car.

DEIRDRE: Turning onto Park.

SCOOPER: Doctor James.

DEIRDRE: He's gone.

SCOOPER: Doctor James.

DEIRDRE: He's gone.

They punch each other. They stab each other. They are weeping and hitting and attacking each other. They stop. They gasp for breath.

SCOOPER: Put down that paper knife. I'm bleeding.

DEIRDRE: Oh dear Christ. I stabbed you. I tried to kill you.

SCOOPER: I ruined your apartment. I tried to kill you!

DEIRDRE: What's the last eight years been for? Are you dying? Are you bleeding?

SCOOPER: Is it all for naught? The last six years? All for naught?

DEIRDRE: The last eight years? All for zero? Have to get out to my father. To read to him.

SCOOPER: It can't be. Back to go. The mother.

DEIRDRE: Back to zero. The father.

CURTAIN

A C T   T W O

———

A hospital room. Henny sits up in the bed. It's two days after the operation. Her I.V. has been disconnected. In spite of her bandaging, it's the first time she's felt comfortable in years. Scooper is a patient in the hospital. He has a bathrobe on over pajamas. His side is bandaged. His arm is bandaged. He sits in a wheelchair.

SCOOPER: Ma, I'm having a lot of trouble relating to people.

HENNY: Every time I call you, you're reading a book. And they're these books no one ever heard of.

SCOOPER: I'm having trouble with women.

HENNY: Don't you ever read anything by a writer who's alive?

SCOOPER: And you are the key woman in my life. The first woman.

HENNY: Writers write books and then they go on promotion tours on the radio and TV and a person like myself who can't read can at least hear about the person who did the writing.

SCOOPER: I would like to examine in this time we have—

HENNY: But you don't read them unless they sold two copies

and been dead nine hundred years and nobody ever made
a movie out of it or heard of it.

SCOOPER: This relationship in a way, a manner, that might
shed light on future relationships with—

HENNY: My friend, Roberta Schildhauer, has always got her
nose in a book. She wore out her library card. They had
to laminate it, and she never heard of any of the stuff
you read.

SCOOPER *holds his side by his spleen. He makes a sudden
retching noise, but then is quiet.*

HENNY: Is that you?

SCOOPER: I got a crick in my side. *He gets out of the wheelchair.*

HENNY: Why did the nurse come and say "Get back in bed."

SCOOPER: There's other people in the room. She was talking to
them.

HENNY: It sounded like she was talking to you.

SCOOPER: Get back to bed? She was being sexy.

HENNY: What does the nurse look like?

SCOOPER: She's the shortest nurse you ever saw with this great
white cap on her head. It looks like this seagull has made
this rest stop on her head on his way out to the horizon.

HENNY: What do you have on?

SCOOPER: Blue striped seersucker suit. Blue shirt. Blue tie with
red apples on it for the Big Apple so they won't tear down
Grand Old Central.

HENNY: You must look nice. No wonder she's being sexy. I'll
get special attention if the nurses know I got a sexy son.

SCOOPER: Henny, you've been lying to me, to yourself for the
past two years. You're going home in ten or twelve days.
I want to make sure you won't ever lie—

HENNY: I wasn't lying—

SCOOPER: You were sick for two years and couldn't trust me. I called you most every day and saw you at Christmas and on your birthday and in all that time you acted like you were sneaking a thermos of martinis onto the beach for daddy to drink.

HENNY: I was going to tell you—

SCOOPER: Tell me what?

HENNY, *sharply:* Tell you I was frightened. What do you think?

SCOOPER: And you couldn't.

HENNY: I couldn't give you my problems.

SCOOPER: You didn't trust me?

HENNY: I was going to call the priest one day and have him come to the house and confess about the sore down there.

SCOOPER: Sores are not sins. Something in you said I do not trust this man who is my son.

HENNY: Did you put the double lock on my apartment? I don't want those people next door raiding my apartment. Oh, the old witch is finally gone. Let's get the furniture. Let's get the dishes. Wheel out the piano.

SCOOPER: Nobody wants anything in that apartment.

HENNY: You do. I'm leaving things for you. I'm collecting sheets for you. I send the girl to open bank accounts and get electric blankets and electric kettles so when you finally get married you'll be all set. You're the only boy on the block with a hope chest.

SCOOPER: I'm not a boy, Henny. I'm forty years old.

HENNY: Forty? Old? You know what old is? When you look back and say Christ, to be seventy-nine again. Nostalgia for eighty. Even eighty-one. That wasn't so bad. To be that young. To be handsome.

SCOOPER: You haven't seen me in years. You don't even know what I look like.

HENNY: You look like Robert Redford.

SCOOPER: You don't know what Robert Redford looks like.

HENNY: He looks like you.

SCOOPER: Henny—

HENNY: The lucky part is I don't know what I look like either.

SCOOPER: The lucky part is this operation—

HENNY *holds her ears:* Don't talk about the operation!

SCOOPER: It was a success.

HENNY: What was a success?

SCOOPER: They got it. You're okay.

HENNY: Between my legs?

SCOOPER: They put a pessary.

HENNY: They put a pet between my legs?

SCOOPER: A silver disc to hold the uterus.

HENNY: My bladder!—

SCOOPER: You don't know. You make everything up for yourself.

HENNY *reaches out her hands:* I can drink water? It won't burn? I want water.

SCOOPER *gives her the pitcher. She takes it and drinks right out of the pitcher. She falls back.*

SCOOPER: The irony is you're probably in the best health you've ever been in in your life. They said for all the neglect, you had the body of a fifty-two-year-old woman.

HENNY: Well, if they find a fifty-two-year-old soul stuck in a six-thousand-year-old body, we can do a complete switch.

SCOOPER: The good thing about being old—

HENNY: Twenty-five-thousand words or less please.

SCOOPER: The cancer moves slow.

HENNY: Stop harping that word!

SCOOPER: They got it. It's out of you. Hallelujah, Saint Jude. Maybe Kotex and Saint Jude are the secret of life. The disease in Fort Bosom is captured. I don't want you leaving this hospital galloping pronto back to the old evasions. Doing anything to avoid hitting center. Not lying. Just evading. I'm talking to myself as well as you. If you're in trouble, you have to tell me.

HENNY: How hot is it in this room? I'm burning up.

SCOOPER: The thermometer here on the window. Eighty-nine degrees.

HENNY: A miracle. An age I haven't been. Pick a number. Any number. I've been it. Who cares how hot it is. I'm in hell and isn't hell supposed to be hot?

SCOOPER: You got yourself in hell all by yourself.

HENNY: And I'll get myself out all by myself.

SCOOPER: Did you show your breast to me—

HENNY: Bosom!

SCOOPER: To stop me from going? I have to know this.

HENNY: Where are you going?

SCOOPER: I was only going away for a few weeks.

HENNY: You going on a trip?

SCOOPER: You had it hidden for two years. Why did you have to pick that time—

HENNY: You can't leave.

SCOOPER: I canceled the trip. Did you know?

HENNY: I'm sorry such a minor thing as this *bosom* incident has fouled up your summer plans.

SCOOPER: Cut the dramatics.

HENNY: I'm eighty-three. I won't be around much longer to screw up your summer vacations. If you write a piece on "My Summer Vacation," don't forget to send me a copy.

I'm learning Braille with my ass. I'll sit on it and learn all I need to know.

SCOOPER: Did you show me your breast to stop me from going?

HENNY: I hate that word. "Breastbeating." Why do you have to use that word, Breast? Sounds like something a chicken has. I always loved my bosoms. Your father loved my bosoms. Bosom buddies. Bosoms are fun. Bosoms are round. I may not have had good legs, or had the straightest teeth, but did my bosoms get attention at the beach. I couldn't wait for summer. I'm a topless dancer now. Half a topless dancer.

SCOOPER: Did you know I was going away?

HENNY: Where are you going? I don't keep track of your life. Who'd tell me?

SCOOPER: Val. Did she let anything slip?

HENNY: I never talk to Valerie.

SCOOPER: She let something slip about a trip?

HENNY: She and Ted sent flowers.

SCOOPER: That we were going away?

HENNY: I wish they sent candy instead. I could eat that bouquet. The food I'll tell you is not so hot here. But don't have them come visit me. They're good friends to you, but I don't want anybody up here seeing me.

SCOOPER: Believe me, they won't be coming.

HENNY: I wish Jack were here. Where is my Jack?

SCOOPER: So you could kill him again?

HENNY: Your father died because he drank and he was drunk all the time and then he drank even more and then he died.

SCOOPER: So why do you wish such a drunk here by your side?

HENNY: To have a man with me.

SCOOPER: You have me.

HENNY: Like I was saying. Where are those nurses? What do

you think Medicare's paying for? I want a cool white towel. Is it daytime? Nighttime? I'm burning up. My head is so ... Scooper? Are you still in the room? *A pause.*

SCOOPER: I'm here.

HENNY: I was going to tell you but I thought how can I tell him with so many worries so deep on his mind? Don't you think I know you're lonely? You got nobody in your life. Things aren't working out. I don't need optometrists to see all that. And now this. Nurses. Me coming home. Who's going to pay for it?

SCOOPER: The Medicare takes it. Relax. When Jack died and you had that suicide—

HENNY: It wasn't suicide. I reached for the wrong pills. I couldn't see. I thought they were breath fresheners. Life Savers.

SCOOPER: Nobody takes eighty-six Life Savers. Nobody's breath is that bad. Jack dying in one hospital. You suiciding in another. Me racing back and forth to see who'd die first. A five-day race. He went. You survived. When it was all over, the Medicare, for some reason I never followed up on, sent me a rebate of forty-four dollars. I made forty-four bucks off the two of you being in the hospital. Who knows what'll happen this time? Jackpot.

HENNY: How did I get in here so quickly? I thought hospitals had waiting lists. I thought you had to wait weeks to get appointments and beds. Three days ago you come see me and that very day I'm taken here and two days ago I'm operated on. How did we get in so quickly?

SCOOPER: It was an emergency.

HENNY: Pearl Harbor is an emergency. An old lady with female problems is no emergency. You didn't have to panic and carry me out.

SCOOPER: You were in pain. Why would you do that to yourself all these years? Put yourself in solitary confinement.

HENNY: Is there anyone else in the room?

SCOOPER: A lady over there. Asleep. Tubes coming out of her. Another lady was here. I guess being operated.

HENNY: Are they ack-blay?

SCOOPER: Both of them.

HENNY: Couldn't you get me a room with ite-whay people in it?

SCOOPER: You're lucky to have this room.

HENNY: Did you stick me on the charity ward?

SCOOPER: It's no charity ward.

HENNY: Let the nurses know I'm somebody. Tell them I am not run of the mill. Tell them I used to be somebody.

SCOOPER: Who did you used to be?

HENNY: Make up somebody. You're the one who reads the books.

SCOOPER: Why don't you ever tell me the truth?

HENNY: Why don't you ever ask me the truth?

SCOOPER: Why did you try to kill yourself ten years ago?

HENNY: Why aren't you married?

SCOOPER: Why did you get married so late?

HENNY: Who is this Doctor James who got me in here?

SCOOPER: A doctor.

HENNY: What kind of a doctor?

SCOOPER: I don't know. He's. They have to be everything.

HENNY: Who does he look like?

SCOOPER: He looks like—believe it or not—he looks like Jack.

HENNY: My Jack? Your father?

SCOOPER: Same slicked-back hair.

HENNY: Your father. So embarrassed about his curls. I said why God wasted curls on you. He said it was a present from heaven: beautiful brains. Doctor James looks like Jack? I can't wait for him to come in again.

SCOOPER: He won't. He's away.

HENNY: Jack could've had anybody. He had me. Biggest shock of my life when he said, Henny, give a guy a break. Marry me. He could've had any girl.

SCOOPER: What did dad mean when he said "That's what I get for marrying a forty-two-year-old virgin." Why would you scream "I can't help it if I'm a good girl." Why would you scream over and over "I can't help it if I'm not a whore like your other women. I can't help it if I kept it for the man I married."

HENNY: I didn't realize I had given birth to a little cassette recorder.

SCOOPER: What kept you two together?

HENNY: I would've called you Xerox, bought stock in you and sold you.

SCOOPER: What was your life like before you married Jack? Before you had me? I'm almost the age you and Jack were when you met. What was your life like?

HENNY: Life like? Life like? Our life was life-like. You like this Doctor James a lot. I can hear a blush in your voice.

SCOOPER: Did you ever have nightmares? You were thirty-eight, thirty-nine, forty. Alone. Unmarried. Not walking the streets like Jack's other girls.

HENNY: Your father and I went to dances.

SCOOPER: Why did two forty-year-old people get married for the first time?

HENNY: To hold up their pants? To get to the other side of the road? I'll bite. Why did two forty-year-old people get married for the first time? We had money to spend on ourselves. We were lonely. Is that a sin? To be lonely. My father had died. I was alone.

SCOOPER: How lonely were you?

HENNY: I met your father in a bar.

SCOOPER: Did it make you wake up in the middle of the night?

HENNY: We'd do this funny dance. I'd pull my bloomers down like a harem girl. We'd do this Egyptian dance.

SCOOPER: My father. Was he lonely?

HENNY: Why would he be lonely?

SCOOPER: You never asked him?

HENNY: I'm supposed to wake him up in the middle of the night and say to my husband I'm lucky to get "Are you lonely?" He'd thwack me in the head. A man is never lonely. A man on his deathbed can pick up the phone and get a date. A woman's different. I had buck teeth. They should've straightened my teeth while I was under the knife. They should've left my bosoms alone and broken my legs and reset them straight. I had grey hair when I was twenty-seven. Too honest to dye it. I made myself attractive telling jokes and acting the life of the party. Slaving in the kitchen. I was always afraid your father would leave. I was glad when he died. The worries were over. He couldn't leave me.

SCOOPER: Then why did you try to kill yourself?

HENNY: What are you? J. Edgar Hoover? Is this the Warren Commission?

SCOOPER: I'm trying to be honest.

HENNY: You just can't start being honest. You don't walk up to a fella and say Hey, today I'm honest.

SCOOPER: There must be something you want to know about me.

HENNY: I'm proud I never pried.

SCOOPER: You never knew how much money your own husband made.

HENNY: I waited for him to tell me.

SCOOPER: You didn't know how old he was.

HENNY: Not my business to ask.

SCOOPER: Your own husband?

HENNY: There was food on the table. You never went hungry.

SCOOPER: He didn't know how old you were.

HENNY: I was older. He would've left me.

SCOOPER: Two years older! Two years!

HENNY: Do they know here? How old I am?

SCOOPER: Your birthday's on your wrist on a little plastic tag.

HENNY: Take it off. Change the date!

SCOOPER: To what?

HENNY: Anything! Make it even older so they'll say I look swell for a ninety-five-year-old woman.

SCOOPER: You're going to die and I'm not going to know anything about you.

HENNY: You know enough about me.

SCOOPER: How you felt?

HENNY, *angry*: Felt? Felt? You make hats out of felt.

SCOOPER: I'm dying I'm so crazy. If I can straighten things out with you, maybe I can do it with all women—

HENNY: Don't you think I know you're unhappy? Don't you think I know that you know that I'm unhappy? You think I tried to kill myself for fun?

SCOOPER: That's the first time I ever heard you admit you tried to kill yourself. Did it hurt? There. That's a start. That's a start.

HENNY: I told the truth. Did the Red Sea part? I'm this old woman who does not want to live in the past and I have this son who is like living in a time capsule. They call it the past because it's over with, done, passed. Bury him with his copy of "Gone With the Wind."

SCOOPER: You're going to be dead and I'm not going to know you.

HENNY: You put me in hospitals.

SCOOPER: Now? You blame me for this?

HENNY: You put me in hospitals before.

SCOOPER: You were crazy. You needed help.

HENNY: Causing blackouts all the electricity they put in me.

SCOOPER: You needed care.

HENNY: Whole coastlines blacked out because of me.

SCOOPER: No one could help you.

HENNY: Major cities. Industry crippled. Airlines. Television. Looting results because of the electricity they put in me to straighten out my head.

SCOOPER: You wouldn't trust anyone.

HENNY: Lot of good it did.

SCOOPER: You wouldn't listen to anyone. You wouldn't ask anyone anything.

HENNY: Okay. Who's this Doctor James that got me in here? I never heard you mention him before. I could hear the blush in your voice. As a kid you were a blusher. You're older. I bet your skin doesn't blush, but my ear is attuned to voices. I can hear the blush in your voice.

SCOOPER: Who do you think he is?

HENNY: What?

SCOOPER: I'm curious to know who you think he is.

HENNY: Twenty Questions? Don't *you* know? I think he's your—

SCOOPER: Speak up. Come on.

HENNY: I don't want the nurses to hear.

SCOOPER: To hear what?

HENNY: I think he's your boyfriend. Am I right?

SCOOPER, *laughing:* Why do you think he's my boyfriend?

HENNY: My friend, Roberta Schildhauer, saw you at East Sixty-eighth Street where she was doing practical nursing across the street for a very wealthy lady and saw you going in and out of the building across the street. She asked the doorman who you went to visit.

SCOOPER: You don't need to see! You have a little blind person's Mafia.

HENNY: She told the doorman you were her daughter's ex-husband and owed alimony. The doorman said you went to see Doctor Virgil James. Roberta asked me who Doctor Virgil James was. I lied to her. I said Oh, an old college chum. They're scribbling away alumni notes.

SCOOPER: Doctor James is a psychiatrist.

HENNY: I know about those shrinkolas. They're all so cuckoo themselves I'm not surprised that's who you got mixed up with. Just don't let him give you drugs. There's nothing those mind shrinkers like better than getting you deep on the drugs. A man was on the Arlene Francis and the Dick Cavett shows talking how those mind shrinkers had screwed him up.

SCOOPER: He's my doctor.

HENNY: This man says in his book they're all junkies themselves.

SCOOPER: My doctor.

HENNY: Why don't you read nice books like that? Books I hear about on the radio that I could talk to you about. *You* needing a psychiatrist? You'd have to be an ingrate! Everything you got. A nice business.

SCOOPER: I'm selling the business. My share to Ted. All over. Finished. Can't work together anymore.

HENNY: Your best friends. Teddy and Valerie. They love you.

SCOOPER: Friends no more.

HENNY: They told me that. They called at Christmas. It's like a home for you.

SCOOPER: Like a home. I want my own home.

HENNY: Never be lonely with friends like that.

SCOOPER: I have been fucking Valerie for the past five years.

HENNY: They sent me flowers.

SCOOPER: She was going to leave Ted but at the last moment she developed this paralysis of the threshold. *Pause.*

HENNY: You and Valerie?

SCOOPER: That's carved on secret trees all over town.

HENNY: What about you and Doctor James?

SCOOPER: I'm his patient. *She puts her hands over her face.* You'd rather I were homosexual than had to go to a doctor?

HENNY: There's nothing sick in being homosexual.

SCOOPER: But going to a psychiatrist?

HENNY: That's sick. SCOOPER *howls.* I love to hear you laugh. When you laugh, the world's back in place. Laughter!! That's the best medicine! Laughter! Doctors know that'll put them out of business! Laugh, Scooper. *Quiet.* Scooper, are you here? *A pause.* Scooper?

SCOOPER: You've been in bug houses. I've had to put you there myself. I've seen you put in the back of trucks and taken away. You're up there in the Loony Hall of Fame. You have gold stars on your strait jackets. I've seen them.

HENNY: And a lot of good it did me. Psychiatrists. My son.

SCOOPER: Six years ago, your son found himself walking bare-foot down Fifth Avenue in the dead of winter carrying a red plastic machine gun. Your son followed a young girl for five blocks because he knew she would be kidnapped and he had to protect her from the aliens who would kill her. Very James Bond. Very Philip Marlowe. Just in the nick of time, your son pulled this girl into a sidestreet to let her know she was protected from those who would do harm to her hair and her skin and her fingernails. She screamed not knowing that your son was her savior. A passer-by heard her scream and grabbed your son. Your son pulled the lit cigarette out of his lips and put it in the Good Samaritan's face. Your son ran down Fifth Avenue

to the Gotham Book Mart that sells old books. Your son
ran into the bookshop to find a different character for himself. Charles Dickens. Something with an eccentricity he
could live with. The police got your son there. Took him
to Bellevue. Thanks to Ted and Valerie, your son got
transferred to the Psychiatric Institute here in this hospital.
Your son's doctor was Doctor James, and he has been my
doctor ever since.

HENNY: Did she press charges?

SCOOPER: No. But a few days later I got a book in the hospital.
"The Letters of Mozart." She had written inside "I am the
girl you attacked. I want you to know I forgive you. Maybe
a little contact with Mozart might heal you."

HENNY: I hope you sent her a thank you note.

SCOOPER: She didn't sign it. I had nowhere to send the letter. I
loved those letters of Mozart.

HENNY *groans:* He loves the letters of Mozart.

SCOOPER: I said for years I look for the perfect girl. One day I
snap. It all goes. I become a mugger. What do I do? I mug
Miss Right. Nowhere to find her. I spent my time going
after women to love them, to chase them, to hassle them,
to talk to them, to touch them, to see them, to smell them,
to feel them, to wound them, to heal them, to taste
them . . .

HENNY: Are you one of those transvestites?

SCOOPER: No, ma.

HENNY: I hear about them on the radio. There's nothing wrong
in being a transvestite.

SCOOPER: I'm trying to clear my life out. I don't want to be
crazy like you.

HENNY: When you were eight years old, you put on my dress.
And my make-up.

SCOOPER: Maybe I was trying to find out who you were.

HENNY: A little Christine Jorgenson. Half man. Half woman. We made a joke. When you were being born we didn't know if we wanted a boy or a girl so we got a little bit of both.

SCOOPER: I have this fantasy that one day you and I will have a scene that will clear everything out between us and I can lay you to rest while you're still alive.

HENNY: Did you have one with your father?

SCOOPER: Yes.

HENNY: Oh no! You couldn't've. He was too busy fighting to share anything. Too busy ripping the tops off beer bottles. Bourbon bottles.

SCOOPER: He had his stroke. I got a cab because that could come quicker than an ambulance.

HENNY: I don't want to hear this.

SCOOPER: He couldn't speak. Left leg couldn't move. Left arm. No voice. We drove up to this hospital. Over the Triborough Bridge. I held him in my arms. "All right, Jack," I said. "All right, dad. Everything is going to be great! Remember when I was a kid, dad, and we'd ride over a bridge and you'd say 'You count all the boats on that side of the bridge, I count 'em on this side, whoever has the most is King for a Day!' Dad, I'll count boats for you. Six. Eight. Nine! You win! You're King for a Day! I love you, Dad." I told him that. I held him. I felt the right side of his body answer me.

HENNY: Then I'll twitch and you can hold me and we'll call it quits.

SCOOPER: Ma, feel these pajamas. Feel this robe. I'm not in a seersucker suit. I'm a patient here. I got stabbed, ma. In the spleen.

HENNY: In the subway! I tell you to ride taxis! I tell you it's dangerous out there—

SCOOPER: No muggers, ma. I tried to hurt somebody again. The words all short-circuited. I didn't mean . . . she didn't mean to.

HENNY: Valerie? Ted stabbed you?

SCOOPER: Deirdre.

HENNY: Deirdre?

SCOOPER: You don't know her.

HENNY: That's what I tell Roberta Schildhauer. You got a million of them.

SCOOPER: Why didn't you trust me? Why didn't you tell me? For two years why didn't you tell me you were standing in front of windows waving statues of impossible saints over you?

HENNY: Where's the spleen?

SCOOPER: I stay away from you because you are all chaos. Your body bursting open. I need my life structured, enclosed. I pick up a book. The page's rectangular shape, obvious but important, *constant* from book to book, dependable, the passion, wisdom, excitement captured in the center of the page tamed by the white margin. I lie on the rectangular couch of Doctor James and yes I become the words on the page. I can face my dreams.

HENNY: Your father and I had that song we'd dance to. "I had a dream, dear, you had one too."

SCOOPER: Ma, I have dreams that you picked me up and used me like a weapon against a strange man.

HENNY: Where's the spleen?

SCOOPER: I feel you holding my feet and my face so close to this strange man and my head is hitting his. My friendships with men are all fucked up. My friendships with women are all fucked up. The doctors say you can't live alone anymore.

HENNY: Doctor James?

SCOOPER: He's away. The surgeon said it.

HENNY: No homes.

SCOOPER: I can't take care of you.

HENNY: Never asked you to.

SCOOPER: Why do you want to stay alive?

HENNY: Did I hear the question right? Why? Why!!!!

SCOOPER: After devoting fifteen solid, very unsolid years to trying to bump yourself off—

HENNY: They were accidents! Household tragedies!

SCOOPER: Now when it's all over are you trying to hang on?

HENNY: It's not all over. You said they got it.

SCOOPER: They got it so it won't kill you immediately. They
didn't go into the lymph glands. You couldn't have stood
up to that. They got rid of the discomfort.

HENNY: How much . . .

SCOOPER: What are you saying?

HENNY: Time.

SCOOPER: He said—

HENNY: Who said?

SCOOPER: The doctor said.

HENNY: I don't want any Doctor James said.

SCOOPER: The surgeon said.

HENNY: Get to it.

SCOOPER: In spite of everything, you were in remarkable health.
He said the cancer—

HENNY: I hate that word.

SCOOPER: Could take ten years till it got you.

HENNY: Ten years?

SCOOPER: Ten years.

HENNY: Ten years! You gotta be joking: ten more years of this?

SCOOPER: Ten more years of this.

HENNY: I must be an awful burden to you.

SCOOPER: You're an awful burden to me. I want to get to a new town, a new country, change the name, you over, start all over again.

HENNY: Ten years.

SCOOPER *very quietly:* Ma. In the drawer of the table to the right of your bed are your pills. Your sleeping pills. I put all your belongings into a plastic bag and put them in that drawer. Ma. You can't live in dignity. You have a chance right now to die in it.

HENNY: You want me to take the pills?

SCOOPER: I want you to take the pills.

HENNY: Are there enough?

SCOOPER: A lot.

HENNY: We'll do it?

SCOOPER: We'll do it.

HENNY: You won't feel badly?

SCOOPER: I won't feel badly.

HENNY: Give me the pills.

SCOOPER *takes the pills out of her bedside table, looking around to make sure no one sees him. He gives her the vial.*

SCOOPER: Ma?

HENNY: Are these the pills?

SCOOPER: I loved you.

HENNY: Is this our scene?

SCOOPER: We'll give each other a hold.

HENNY: Don't do that. It hurts.

SCOOPER: Your hand.

HENNY: Where's your hand? *They connect hands.*

SCOOPER: Thank you.

HENNY: Thank you?

SCOOPER: For life. Caring for me.

HENNY: Oh, that.

SCOOPER: We'll forgive each other.

HENNY: You won't get into trouble over this?

SCOOPER: With your history?

HENNY: I don't want you getting into any trouble for this.

SCOOPER: Open your hands. *He pours the pills in.*

HENNY: Give me water. *He pours her water. She drinks.* I'll need lots of water. It feels like a lot there. It's so exciting to drink water again. *She shakes the vial.* You're sure you won't get in trouble for this?

SCOOPER: I'll stay by your side. You'll fall asleep.

HENNY: To drink water and not have it burn.

SCOOPER: I'm by your side.

HENNY: Water shouldn't burn.

SCOOPER: Still. Quiet.

HENNY: 350-2219. That's the butcher. He delivers. If you ever want anything delivered.

SCOOPER: 350-2219.

HENNY: I keep a hundred numbers right up here in my head.

SCOOPER: I loved you.

HENNY: I loved your father.

SCOOPER: Thank you. That's important to know.

HENNY: I love you.

SCOOPER: Goodbye.

HENNY: You sure you'll light a lot of candles for me?

SCOOPER: They'll see the glow in Helena, Montana.

HENNY: When I was a little girl, I dreamed of being a great actress and I would change my name to Helena Montana.

SCOOPER: Your own name is all right.

HENNY: Goodbye.

SCOOPER: Goodbye.

HENNY *flings the pills across the room:* You rotten little shit, do you think they're going to let me bring killer pills in here? These are for my gas. You'd have done it? You'd have let me die?

SCOOPER: Take these pills! *He picks them off the floor.*

HENNY: Nurse! Nurse!

SCOOPER: Quiet. *He turns to the door. He speaks to the nurse.* She's all right. Was dreaming. *A pause. He waits for the nurse to leave. He sits by her bed.* I want you dead.

HENNY: God help me if I get gas in this hospital. *She tosses the empty vial away.*

SCOOPER: What keeps you alive?

HENNY: You. I want to know what happens to you.

SCOOPER: I want to kill you.

HENNY: That interests me.

SCOOPER: I want you to die.

HENNY: That, my God, amazes me.

SCOOPER: Nothing's working out for me.

HENNY, *thrilled*: I know.

SCOOPER: What am I going to do? I put all this time into Valerie.

HENNY: That's what I want to know about.

SCOOPER *sits in his wheelchair*: What am I telling you? You can't help me.

HENNY: I'm not trying to.

SCOOPER: Ma, I'm not a book you sit there passively and keep turning the pages.

HENNY: Oh yes, you are. You're my book. The day the nurse put you in my arms, I looked down at you. This complete stranger had come out of me. That I could produce this stranger. Would you take my breast? Would you drink? Would you live? Would you die? Would you be run over? Would you get polio or crib death or meningitis or be kidnapped? Would you learn? Who would you look like?

You've always come up trumps, Scooper. Just when I'm about to give up on you and I say I knew what that boy is all about, out of the blue, I realize you're trying to kill me. That's so exciting. And to find out about you and Valerie! You could knock me over. Will she leave? Will she stay with Ted? How will Ted take it? Can you even keep Valerie? You want me to be open? Here I am. Open. *Silence.* But you're not ready to be. Poor Scooper.

SCOOPER: I'm not Scooper. My name is James.

HENNY: Now see that. I wondered how long you want to keep being called Scooper.

SCOOPER: You named me!

HENNY: I beg to differ. You were always scooping sand and putting it in your bucket. I said "You're like a little ostrich scooping sand for his head." You said "Scooper!" "Scooper!" You made us call you Scooper. If we wouldn't call you Scooper, you wouldn't come. It's awful having a kid with a silly name like Scooper. It could've been worse. You could've wanted to be called Ostrich. People would look at me as if actually calling another human being Scooper was my idea. Not my idea! His idea. Scooper. No wonder nobody can take you seriously. Or trust you. This is so interesting. I was wondering when you'd get around to changing your name back to what we named you. James! After my father. A wonderful man. James. The first. You're James the Second.

DEIRDRE *appears in the door. She has a robe over her hospital gown and hobbles in on crutches.*

DEIRDRE: I called my father.

HENNY: Who's there?

DEIRDRE: I said a man tried to kill me.

HENNY: Who is that?

DEIRDRE: I said it fast so he wouldn't hang up on me. He didn't speak but he didn't hang up. I poured it all out. I told him I was in the hospital and I wouldn't be out to see him for a few days and finally he spoke to me. He said "Give me his name. I will tell certain men to see him."

HENNY: Get out of my room. My son and I are—

DEIRDRE: "You don't touch a hair on the head of my Deirdre of the Sorrows." He said that.

HENNY: Is this for you, Scooper?

SCOOPER: Yes, ma.

DEIRDRE: I said "Poppa, that's a play by John Millington Synge." He said "I named you after that play. Didn't I ever tell you?" He's going to kill you.

HENNY: Girl trouble?

SCOOPER: Yes, ma.

HENNY: Scooper! *She leans forward, concentrating intently, eyes closed shut.*

DEIRDRE: He's going to send people out, find you and kill you for hurting the daughter of the professor. We talked! My father and I *talked*.

HENNY: Say something, Scooper!

SCOOPER: I think you're going to extremes. I'm very happy you and your father—

DEIRDRE *hits the wheels of his chair with her crutches:* Don't even mention him.

SCOOPER: You don't have to operate out of his code.

DEIRDRE: My father and I connected.

SCOOPER: You don't have to kill me to make up for all the years he didn't pay any attention to you.

DEIRDRE: I don't want his name in your mouth!

SCOOPER: You of all people should understand panic and losing control.

DEIRDRE: You did something worse. Worse than hitting me.

SCOOPER: You stabbed me.

HENNY: Stabbed! Scooper, this is wonderful!

DEIRDRE: Worse than making me stab you. Worse than screwing up Doctor James for me.

SCOOPER: In a way we had a wonderful afternoon. I had hoped we'd—

DEIRDRE: We'd what? You had your chance. You had me. You touched me. You dropped me.

SCOOPER: And you're going to have me killed?

DEIRDRE: You made me afraid. I want to find Doctor James. I want him to see you for what you are.

HENNY: Doctor James again! The Mystery Man!

SCOOPER: In a month you can tell him all.

DEIRDRE: Oh, I'll tell him all. He'll throw you out in the gutter if you ever show up there again.

SCOOPER: Tell him whatever you want. It's one way to finish with Doctor James.

DEIRDRE *hits the wheels of his chair with her crutches:* Don't you say one word against him.

SCOOPER: I don't know where he is.

DEIRDRE: How am I going to get through this goddam month?

SCOOPER: I could put an emergency call into the AMA.

DEIRDRE, *rhetorically:* Who said April was the cruelest month?

SCOOPER: T. S. Eliot.

DEIRDRE: August. August. August.

HENNY: I know where he is. *A pause.*

DEIRDRE: Who is this woman?

HENNY: Hi! I'm him. But I don't want to butt in.

SCOOPER: What do you mean? You know where he is.

HENNY: When you went to check me in, we stood out on the sidewalk. Talk about heat. Sidewalks buckling beneath me. This strange hand holding on to me. I don't know where I am.

SCOOPER: What did he say?

HENNY: Don't get on the bed! You're worse than a cat! *Scooper backs off.* Is there such a place as Haiti?

DEIRDRE: Doctor James is in Haiti?

SCOOPER: Are you making this up?

HENNY: No! We were making conversation. I said New York's like a jungle. He said I'm going to the jungle. A big white hotel. Talk about creepy.

SCOOPER: Haiti! I could go there.

DEIRDRE: Haiti. I could go there.

SCOOPER: Talk to him.

DEIRDRE: Explain to him.

SCOOPER: He'd want to see me.

DEIRDRE: He'd weep to see me.

SCOOPER: I have the tickets.

DEIRDRE: I'll call my travel agent.

SCOOPER: I have the reservations at the same hotel. *He takes his wallet out. He fishes out the airline tickets.*

DEIRDRE: Fly down. See him. Fly right back. I could swing that.

SCOOPER: Take one ticket.

DEIRDRE: I don't want anything from you.

SCOOPER: Don't let it go to waste.

DEIRDRE *takes the ticket:* I'll pay you later.

SCOOPER: Fine.

DEIRDRE: I don't want any free rides.

SCOOPER: And none of us will ever get them.

DEIRDRE: He'll help us. He'll help *you.*

SCOOPER: He'll help you.

DEIRDRE: And I'm doomed to travel with you? It's like some plot.

SCOOPER: Shoes like a C.I.A. agent. Not one crease in them. Silently sliding through our lives . . . my God! You don't think—

DEIRDRE: It *is* a plot? You never mentioned to him you were going to Haiti?

SCOOPER: Haiti never came up.

DEIRDRE: And yet he knows. He's planned to drive us crazy all along. And bring us down there. He's arranged all this. Maybe he did it unconsciously. Even a shrink can have a subconscious. Doctor James is sitting under a palm tree. We're face to face. Finally. "So our little odyssey has brought us to the jungle . . ."

SCOOPER: What is he trying to do to us?

DEIRDRE: That devil—

SCOOPER: That evil—

DEIRDRE: Diabolical.

SCOOPER: No. Good.

DEIRDRE: Wonderful.

SCOOPER: See him!

DEIRDRE: Face him! Knock on the door of his hotel room. She'll answer the door. "Oh, hello Mrs. James, may I see the doctor? It's Deirdre."

SCOOPER: "Hi Doctor. It's Scooper."

DEIRDRE: Scooper?

HENNY: Scooper. His name is Scooper. Not my idea.

DEIRDRE: I can't go into the jungle with anyone named Scooper.

HENNY: It's a nickname for James.

DEIRDRE: Your name is James? *Pause.*

SCOOPER: I never made the connection!!!! Doctor James. Me James.

DEIRDRE, *in awe:* You've done it. You have devoured Dr. James. He is in you. The transference is complete. His wisdom has unlocked your wisdom. James. James!!!! How lucky you are. *She turns to go.* Goodbye. *Pause.*

SCOOPER: Jane Bowles is neglected.

DEIRDRE, *stopping—but not turning:* Carson McCullers.

SCOOPER: Joyce Carol Oates.

DEIRDRE, *turning:* How can you say she's neglected? She writes a book a week.

SCOOPER: I never read them.

DEIRDRE: A neglected author is not one you choose to neglect. *She turns to go.*

SCOOPER: Joseph Conrad.

DEIRDRE: "Chance"?

SCOOPER: "Sacred call of life." Page 452.

DEIRDRE: Page 452. "The greatest sin to resist the embrace."

SCOOPER: Are we that couple?

DEIRDRE: I can't. I can't keep starting . . .

SCOOPER: Your father—was he really in the Mafia?

DEIRDRE: He's a librarian.

SCOOPER: What's your truth?

DEIRDRE: Like everyone else's. Sordid, banal—of interest only to myself.

SCOOPER: Tell me one truth.

DEIRDRE: New York really is empty in August. *Pause.*

SCOOPER *stands.* DEIRDRE *motions him not to disturb Henny, who has fallen asleep.* SCOOPER *gestures to go outside. He pushes his wheelchair to the bed.* SCOOPER *and* DEIRDRE *go out.* HENNY *wakes.*

HENNY: James? James? Is she gone? Take my hand, James? *Pause.* O.K. Play the Quiet Man. Hearing the name James over and over, I keep thinking of my father. He was a wonderful man. After he died, I was lost. His dying broke me in about a million pieces but after a while I pasted myself together into some kind of new tea cup and toddled off to Boston for a new drink of water. I loved Boston. They laughed at my New York accent. It made me stand out. I met a man. Don Walker. He was Amish. I said "You must be nuts to love me." He said "No, because I have all my buttons." I said "Which makes you ex-Amish, seeing as how you are not allowed to have buttons." And he said, "Well, you're no great shakes," and I said "Neither are you or you'd still be a Shaker." Believe me, it was funny at the time. We loved each other. I felt my father in heaven was paying attention to me and had sent Don to me as a heavenly present. But Don's Quaker mother who unfortunately was still on this earth would not have her precious ex-Amish son hitched up with a shanty Irish Catholic girl from Manhattan. Even though we were *very* lace curtain. Maybe rayon curtain. But not shanty. Not trash. But only a Quaker girl was good enough for her son. He buckled under. Stopped calling me. Neglected to keep dates. I got the message. I moved my broken tea cup of heart back to New York. Moved into 214 Riverside Drive. Met your father in the lobby. One disappointed person? Meet another disappointed person. Years went by. We got married. To show we could. We stayed together. We had you. And one day I dressed you up and got on the morning train to Boston. I waited outside my old office on Summer Street until Don Walker came out for lunch. I acted like I was just passing by. I wanted it to seem like I had just bumped into him, act casual, show him how great my life was, show off my beautiful child that was not his. And I saw him and I loved him so much. And after we said hellos and fancy meeting yous and acted surprised, I picked you up to show him what he missed and instead I hit him with you. Because he wasn't your father. Because he hadn't trusted me. Because I hadn't meant enough to him. I kept hitting him with you, pushing your face into his, till I realized your nose was bleeding. He was so shocked. I kept saying "You neglected me." I kept screaming like some shanty Irish Banshee: "I loved you." Finally he ran off. I wiped off your face. We got back on the next train to New York. Your father was home. He didn't ask why we were late, what we had done. He read his paper. Had his drinks. Slept. I put you to bed. I took off all my clothes and stood in front of the mirror. This body was not good enough. It couldn't get me what I wanted . . . maybe if . . . maybe . . . I got dressed. Sat by your bed. Stared and stared at you. This was my prayer. A better life for you. You woke up. You looked at me. I want that for you. I want that for you . . . James?

She reaches out for her son.

CURTAIN